Germany

Polity Histories series

Ali M. Ansari, *Iran*
Adrian Bingham, *United Kingdom*
Kerry Brown, *China*
Emile Chabal, *France*
Alan Dowty, *Israel*
Jeff Kingston, *Japan*
David W. Lesch, *Syria*
Dmitri Trenin, *Russia*
Joel Wolfe, *Brazil*

Germany

Andrew I. Port

polity

First published in 2025 by Polity Press Ltd.

Polity Press Ltd.
65 Bridge Street
Cambridge CB2 1UR, UK

Polity Press Ltd.
111 River Street
Hoboken, NJ 07030, USA

ISBN-13: 978-1-5095-4666-4
ISBN-13: 978-1-5095-4667-1 (pb)

A catalogue record for this book is available from the British Library.

Library of Congress Control Number: 2025934600

Typeset in 11 on 13 Berkeley by
Cheshire Typesetting Ltd, Cuddington, Cheshire
Printed and bound in Great Britain by Ashford Colour Ltd

For further information on Polity, visit our website:
politybooks.com

For Peter, Eva, and Beate
"Between Cossacks and Cowboys"

Contents

Preface

Thanks to good fortune, I found myself in West Berlin the night the Wall fell, having arrived three weeks earlier with plans to learn more about modern German history. I spent the next two years doing just that, financing my studies at the Free University (its name notwithstanding) by working as a bartender for the US Army, which, along with British, French, and Soviet forces, still occupied Berlin more than forty years after the end of World War II. As fate would have it, I wound up doing more than just mixing drinks and studying history – I got to experience the latter firsthand!

Living history in such a dramatic and positive way was what convinced me to become a professional historian. Simply put, I wanted to bring the past alive for others, and I hope I've managed to do that with this book, the product and distillation of decades of study. When publisher Louise Knight first approached me about contributing to her new series, "Polity Histories," she encouraged me to write a short, accessible, and "vibrant" book that would appeal to readers who wished to acquaint themselves quickly with contemporary Germany. I hope the book meets her expectations, but that it also includes observations and insights of interest and value to those with greater knowledge of the postwar period. In accordance with the series guidelines and target audience, I have kept endnotes to a minimum. Readers who wish to learn more about the individual topics and themes I cover are encouraged to consult the bibliographical essay.

The most gratifying task of writing a book comes at its completion, when one has the opportunity to thank those individuals who helped make it possible in the first place. The staff at Polity could not have been more supportive and patient. My heartfelt thanks to Louise and her dedicated colleagues: Julia Davies, Evie Deavall, Olivia Jackson, Inès Boxman, Jane Fricker, and the anonymous reviewers. My gratitude as well to Katja Hering at the German Historical Institute in Washington, DC, who kindly helped with the maps. Last but not least, I would like to thank my wife, fellow historian Sylvia Taschka, and our daughters, Hannah Port and Rebekka Port. Without their love and support in an increasingly dark time, this book would never have seen the light of day.

The German Empire, 1871–1918

Source: *German History in Documents and Images (GHDI)*, rev., exp. ed., vol. 4, ed. J. Retallack. Original cartography: Cherie Norton/Mapping Solutions/James Retallack, rev. cartography Gabriel Moss, 2021. https://germanhistorydocs.org/en/forging-an-empire-bismarckian-germany-1866-1890/the-german-empire-1871-1918.

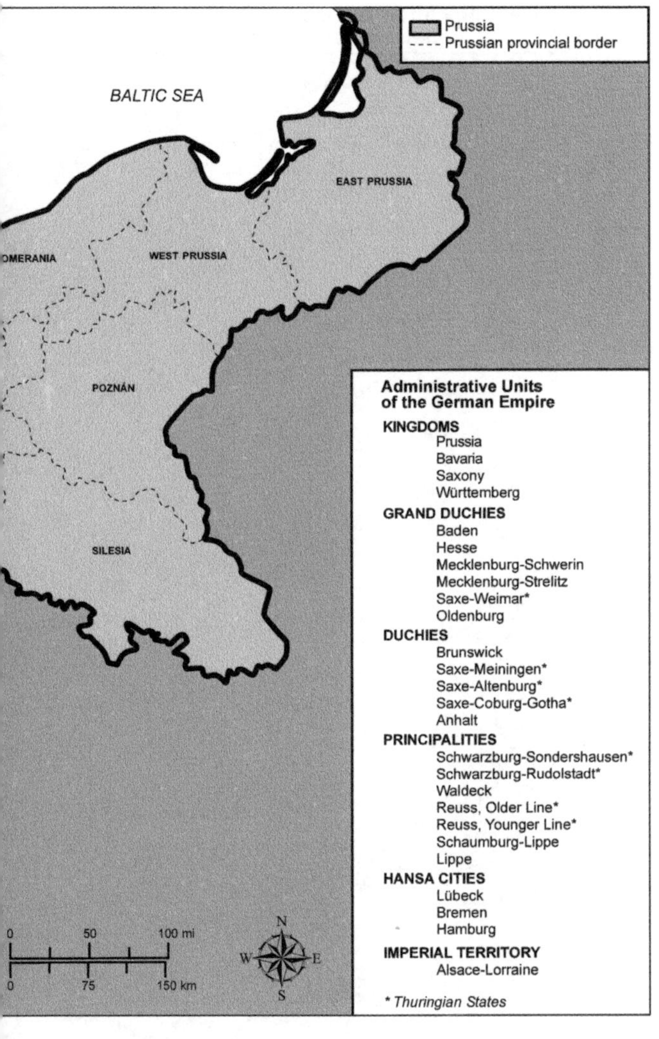
Prussia
Prussian provincial border
BALTIC SEA
EAST PRUSSIA
WEST PRUSSIA
OMERANIA
POZNÁN
SILESIA
0
50
100 mi
0
75
150 km
N
W
E
S
Administrative Units of the German Empire
KINGDOMS
Prussia
Bavaria
Saxony
Württemberg
GRAND DUCHIES
Baden
Hesse
Mecklenburg-Schwerin
Mecklenburg-Strelitz
Saxe-Weimar*
Oldenburg
DUCHIES
Brunswick
Saxe-Meiningen*
Saxe-Altenburg*
Saxe-Coburg-Gotha*
Anhalt
PRINCIPALITIES
Schwarzburg-Sondershausen*
Schwarzburg-Rudolstadt*
Waldeck
Reuss, Older Line*
Reuss, Younger Line*
Schaumburg-Lippe
Lippe
HANSA CITIES
Lübeck
Bremen
Hamburg
IMPERIAL TERRITORY
Alsace-Lorraine
* Thuringian States

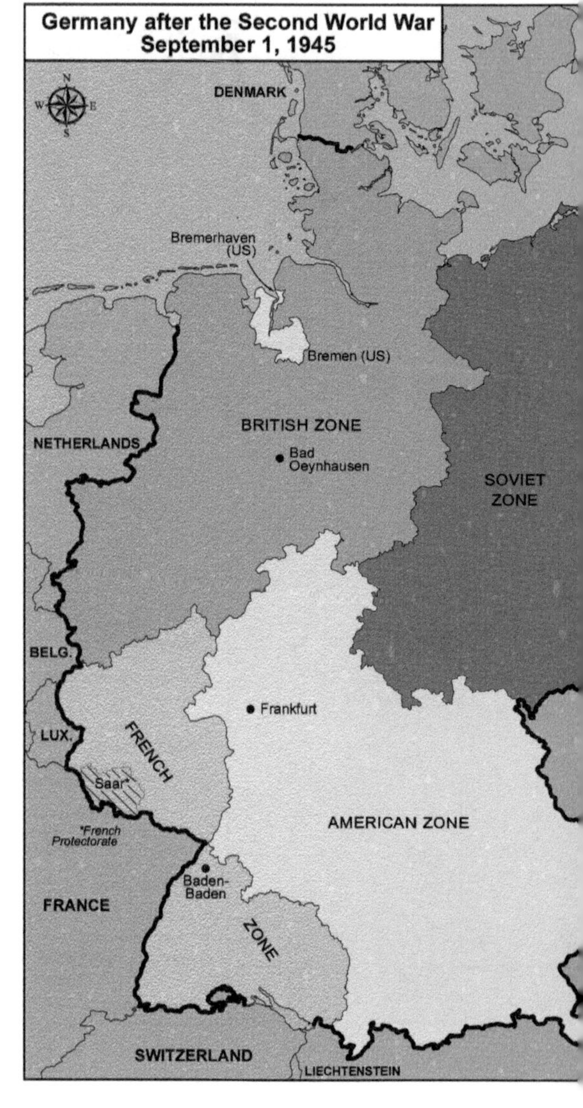
Germany after the Second World War
September 1, 1945
N
S
E
W
DENMARK
Bremerhaven (US)
Bremen (US)
BRITISH ZONE
NETHERLANDS
Bad Oeynhausen
SOVIET ZONE
BELG.
Frankfurt
LUX.
FRENCH
Saar*
AMERICAN ZONE
*French Protectorate
Baden-Baden
FRANCE
ZONE
SWITZERLAND
LIECHTENSTEIN

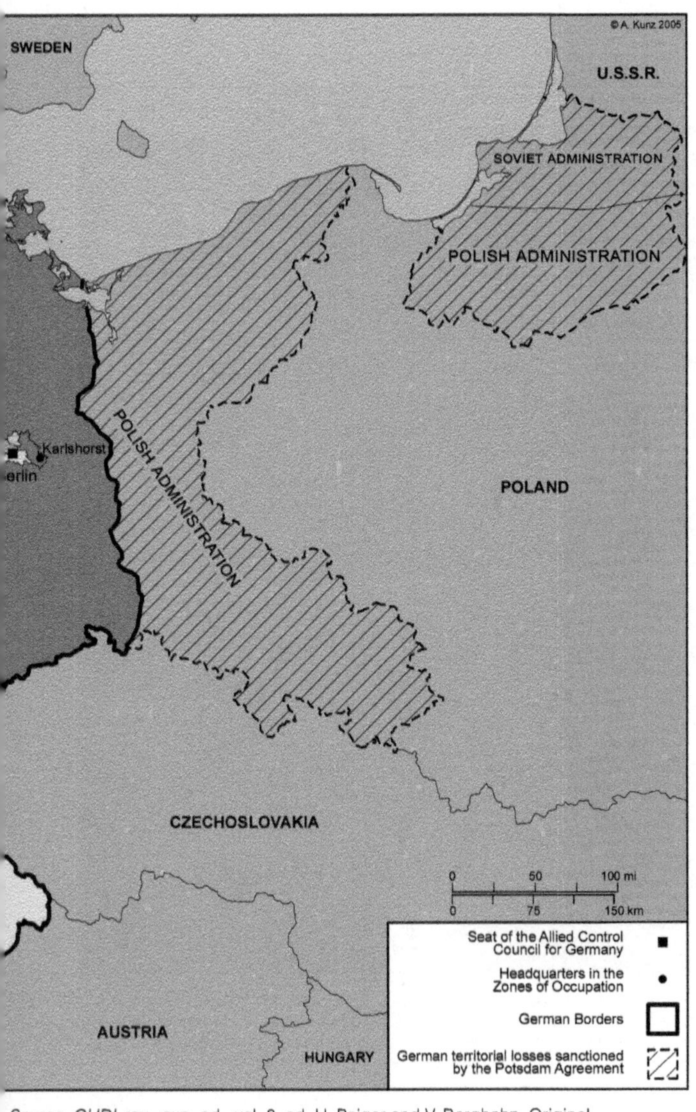

Source: *GHDI*, rev., exp. ed., vol. 8, ed. U. Poiger and V. Berghahn. Original cartography: IEG-MAPS, Mainz/A. Kunz /J.R. Moeschl, rev. cartography Gabriel Moss, 2021. https://germanhistorydocs.org/en/occupation-and-the-emergence-of-two-states-1945-1961/germany-after-the-second-world-war-september-1-1945.

Source: *GHDI*, rev., exp. ed., vol. 10, ed. K. Jarausch and H. Welsh. Original cartography: IEG-MAPS, Mainz/A. Kunz/J.R. Moeschl, rev. cartography Gabriel Moss, 2022. https://germanhistorydocs.org/en/a-new-germany-1990-2023/states-of-the-federal-republic-december-31-1990.

Introduction

Let us imagine a woman, born in early 1890 somewhere in recently unified Germany. After living a hundred years, she passes away peacefully in the winter of 1990. This centenarian could conceivably have known no fewer than six different Germanies: Otto von Bismarck's *Kaiserreich* (German Empire), an authoritarian monarchy that lasted until the end of World War I; the Weimar Republic, the first democracy on German soil; Adolf Hitler's fascist Third Reich, a totalitarian dictatorship that ended with another, this time genocidal, world war; the German Democratic Republic (GDR), a repressive communist regime installed and propped up by the Soviet Union; the liberal-democratic state of West Germany, an integral member of the postwar Western alliance; and, finally, a sovereign and "reunified" Federal Republic.

Depending on her place of birth, mobility might have become the woman's lot in life beginning in the 1940s. Had she grown up, say, in the easternmost provinces of Prussia – in what is today Poland – there is a good chance she would have been one of the millions of ethnic Germans expelled by Polish authorities beginning in the waning months of the war. After trekking hundreds of miles westward, perhaps with her children or grandchildren in tow, she might have eventually settled in the eastern half of Berlin, which became the capital of communist East Germany in 1949.

A decade later, she might have decided to pack up and surreptitiously leave for the West – along with the nearly 3 million other East Germans who fled to the Federal Republic before communist authorities erected the infamous Berlin Wall in the summer of 1961. The woman would have been a pensioner by this point, content perhaps to live out her remaining years in prosperous West Germany. Fortunate and hardy, she would have witnessed the fall of the Wall in her final year of life and then, less than twelve months later, the unification of the two postwar German states on October 3, 1990.

This woman would have lived under vastly different state formations, from constitutional monarchy and parliamentary democracy to the destructive political and economic systems that developed in response to the challenges of modernity: fascism and communism. There has been much debate about what, if anything, makes Germany special or different from other leading industrial nations. Serving as a laboratory for so many different forms of government is surely one notable feature of its modern history. But most interest in Germany tends to focus instead on the Third Reich, World War II, and the Holocaust.

The country's rich, thousand-year history should not be reduced to, *cannot* be boiled down to, the dozen years lasting from 1933 to 1945 – though a quick glance at the European history section of most bookstores usually suggests otherwise. This is not to question the central importance of those fateful years, which, for understandable reasons, cast a long shadow across the eight decades since Hitler committed suicide in his Berlin bunker in the final days of the war – *and* across earlier centuries as well. Long after the end of World War II, the barbaric crimes committed by the Nazis continue to color perceptions and self-perceptions of the country, its people, and its history. Yet, the story of how Germans managed to put their violent, genocidal past behind them and create a stable and prosperous democracy reluctant to use force and committed to the defense of human rights – that, too, is an important and gripping tale.

To their credit, most historians worth their salt steer clear nowadays of simplistic narratives that suggest some sort of straight line from Martin Luther, the father of the Reformation, to Bismarck, the midwife of German unity, to Hitler, the architect of Germany's murderous self-destruction. But there is still a tendency to interpret an entire millennium through the lens of a fateful dozen years. This leads to unnecessary distortions and historical deformations.

For one, it makes it extremely difficult to account for the vastly different path Germans have taken since 1945. Just as important, it has bogged us down in stale debates about "national characters," "special paths," and "German Questions" – all in a seemingly futile attempt to explain the inexplicable, namely this: How was one of the world's most "civilized" and "advanced" nations – the same "land of poets and thinkers" that gave the world Bach and Kant, Goethe and Marx, Freud and Einstein – capable of committing some of the most benighted and inhumane acts in human history? In other words, what went "wrong" – and why?

One of the least satisfying responses to that intractable question offers dubious claims about the German "national character." The "orderly and efficient" denizens of Europe's "land in the middle" were, we are told, rabidly militaristic and nationalistic, insecure about their nation's standing but inordinately apolitical, rigidly bureaucratic, and excessively obedient to authority. Like the parable of the blind men and the elephant, such generalizations only focus on specific aspects of the whole, usually taken out of context. For that reason, they singularly fail to capture the "reality" and "essence" of Germans and Germany – as if such things actually existed. After all, are these the same "apolitical" and "obedient" Germans who rose up and revolted in 1848, 1918, 1953, in the first mass uprising in the Soviet bloc, and then, most successfully, in 1989, helping to bring the Cold War to a close?

Claims about social and political "backwardness" – as opposed to cultural and economic dynamism – ring equally hollow. In contrast to "model" places in the West, like Britain and France, German history was supposedly a series of wrong turns, failures, and deviations. A "belated" or "latecomer" nation, Germany embarked on a "special path" devoid of sound civic virtues and a strong middle class, a place where "traditional" – that is, conservative – social and political structures proved stubbornly resilient, producing an especially destructive clash with the forces of modernity. Its parliament, the Reichtag, may have introduced universal manhood suffrage to continental Europe in 1871, but power remained firmly in the hands of the old elites – including the reactionary Junker, the landowning, neo-feudal nobility of eastern Prussia who dominated the military, civil service, and diplomatic corps.

Since the 1970s and 1980s, historians have distanced themselves from such claims, offering a more nuanced portrait of imperial Germany. Instead, a new paradigm has quietly, almost imperceptibly taken hold in recent years: an assumption that the rapidity and simultaneity of modernity's major ruptures – industrialization and urbanization, for example, the rise of mass politics and class warfare – were somehow more pronounced in Germany than elsewhere, and that it was this that led to especially explosive clashes at home and abroad. A similar type of argument tries to account for the fateful collapse of Germany's first democracy, the result of a "peculiar combination of long-term and short-term pressures," common to all industrial countries at the time, but that "came together with particular force in Weimar Germany."[1] Perhaps.

Whatever their (de)merits, all these approaches are attempts to answer the vexed "German Question," which has taken many shapes and been asked in various ways since the mid-nineteenth century – beginning with domestic debates over the "proper" way to achieve German unity. Those discussions have been closely bound up with questions about German "identity." What is German? What and *where* is Germany? Language and culture, values and beliefs, common traditions and historical experiences all provide clues, but only *inexact* ones, given intense regional and linguistic differences that go back a millennium, long before the advent of modern means of communication and education.

Following the wars of German unification in the 1860s and the country's subsequent emergence as a major military and industrial power, the focus of the "German Question" shifted more to the perspective of outsiders, who wanted to ensure that a powerful Germany not pose a threat to its neighbors. What, with an eye to European and later global harmony, was the nation's "proper" place and role on the international stage? That question became even more pressing after the carnage of the two world wars and National Socialism, but it seemed to be settled in the late 1940s, at least provisionally, when Germany was divided once again – this time into two states belonging to two rival military alliances.

***

If the driving question about the years prior to 1945 has long been a disheartening one – "Where did Germany go wrong?" – the period since the war presents us with a different puzzle, a new German Question: How and why did Germany "go right"?[2] After 1989 and the collapse of communism, Cassandras at home and abroad feared that the hoary German Question would return with a vengeance, that a newly aggressive Germany was looming on the horizon. That has not been the case, yet. Just the opposite, in fact, to the chagrin of the country's closest allies, who often wish the Germans would "do more" when it comes to joint military efforts in the international arena. Such concerns seem more urgent instead when it comes to the *domestic* aspect of the thorny German Question, that is, to issues related to internal unity. Continuing tensions and divisions between the postwar eastern and western halves – between so-called *Ossis* and *Wessis* – are the most current incarnation of that perennial bugbear.

To get at these fundamental issues, this book takes an integrative approach that examines the histories of the two postwar German states in tandem – instead of in isolation, with one chapter on West Germany, for example, the next on the GDR. That customary approach usually involves an emphasis on their obvious differences. In brief, the East German dictatorship lacked all those things that characterized the Federal Republic and other liberal-democratic states and pluralistic societies in the West: due process and democratic elections; a largely unfettered market economy; an independent judiciary, uncensored media, and guarantees of basic civil rights.

But comparisons that explore the neglected or unexpected similarities between the two postwar Germanies can be equally fruitful and revealing. That there were such similarities should not be altogether surprising. After all, even with strong regional variations, both halves shared many political, socioeconomic, and cultural traditions. And, at the outset of the postwar period, they faced a number of similar challenges as a result of wartime destruction. All of this makes the two postwar Germanies a valuable case study, or "laboratory," for examining in a comparative manner the ways in which the capitalist West and communist East faced these as well as other challenges common to all modern, industrialized societies. At the same time, it helps us understand better what worked and what did not, and why that was the case.

This was a flawed "experiment," of course, because the two states were not kept in strict isolation, no matter how hard the East German leadership may have tried! In fact, policies in one state often had a direct or indirect influence on those adopted on the other side of the Elbe River that separated them. Just as important, there were remarkably similar social developments in the two postwar states, though often for vastly different reasons. This is important for understanding the period after unification in 1990. Just as their many *dis*similarities lay at the heart of the difficult and painful process of unification, their oft-neglected similarities help explain why the new Federal Republic has enjoyed such relative success and stability over the past three and a half decades. Considering both sides of the equation helps us gauge whether it is likely to do so for the foreseeable future.

A Thousand Years

There are many ways to approach – and thereby impose some semblance of order on – the grand sweep of German history. *One* device is through the lens of disunity and the millennium-long struggle to overcome that divisive state of affairs. During the Cold War, the country's separation into two states was considered an anomaly, though one that most *West* Germans had come to accept and view as "normal" by the late 1980s – or at least not likely to change much in the foreseeable future.[3] It was not. For almost a thousand years, division and territorial fragmentation seemed to be the lot of the Germanic-speaking population of Central Europe, beginning with the Holy Roman Empire, which came into being three centuries after its predecessor and namesake had collapsed in the West. Resurrected by Charlemagne in the year 800 CE and later rechristened by his successors, the new creation had a highly decentralized structure for much of its existence. Nominally ruled by a distant Kaiser, or emperor, it was essentially a loose cluster of autonomous states that ranged in size from powerful kingdoms like Swabia and Saxony to tiny principalities, bishoprics, and proud "free cities" like Halberstadt and Hamburg.

In the early sixteenth century, in the wake of the challenge Luther's Reformation posed to united Christendom, those divisions became even more entrenched – and violent, triggering a cascade of religious clashes that culminated in 1618, with the outbreak of the Thirty Years' War. That conflict, one of the bloodiest and most destructive in European history, began as a religious struggle between Protestant and Catholic German princes but quickly escalated into an international *political* showdown among the leading powers of Europe. The French, Swedes, and others laid waste to the region for three decades, treating it as a personal plaything in pursuit of their own particular ambitions.

When fighting finally ended in 1648 with the signing of the Peace of Westphalia, the carnage was over. Yet the German-speaking lands of Central Europe remained as territorially fragmented as ever, this time primarily along religious lines, with an individual ruler's faith determining that of his state. The treaty formally introduced the concept of state sovereignty, a novel principle that became entrenched during the so-called Age of Absolutism of the seventeenth and eighteenth centuries. Monarchs throughout Europe consolidated their power during this period – including the rulers of Prussia and Austria, the two largest and most powerful of the roughly 1,800 states that made up the Holy Roman Empire *of the German Nation*, its new appellation since the eve of the Reformation.

The royal Hohenzollern–Habsburg rivalry for control and influence over the German-speaking lands was *the* story of the mid-nineteenth century, from the end of the Napoleonic Wars in 1815 to the partial unification of those states in 1871. Few might have guessed at that confrontation, given the humiliating military defeats both states initially suffered at the hands of Napoleon, who effectively dissolved the Holy Roman Empire in 1806.

French foreign aggression in the wake of the country's 1789 revolution first lit the spark of modern German nationalism, and, over the decades following the Congress of Vienna, calls for greater unity became increasingly common. Inspired by revolutionary developments in neighboring France, liberals – primarily students and members of the educated middle classes – hoped to replace German regionalism (*Kleinstaaterei*) with a single polity. This culminated in the revolution of 1848, memorably described by one historian as a "turning point" that "failed to turn."[4] A national assembly met in the city of Frankfurt, where its members adopted a constitution that embodied classic liberal demands, including representative political institutions and guarantees of basic civil rights and freedoms. But the Prussian and Austrian monarchs put the kibosh on their efforts, summarily rejecting the document and ordering their armies to disperse the parliament and put down all lingering revolutionary remnants.

Middle-class efforts to overcome German particularism failed, but developments initiated at the time from on high nevertheless moved in that direction. This included Prussia's creation of a Customs Union (*Zollverein*) in 1834. The Hohenzollern state excluded Austria and the Habsburgs' vast, non-ethnic German territories from that economic body, an omen of what was to come three decades later, when a series of wars finally brought about German unity – or at least one iteration of that goal. In the 1860s, a constitutional spat between the Prussian monarch and parliament brought to power Otto von Bismarck, an arch-conservative member of the civil service nobility and landowning Junker class. Infamously declaring that the "great issues of the day" would be decided by "blood and iron" (thereby cementing Prussia's already militarist reputation), Bismarck instigated a series of three wars – first against Denmark in 1864, then Austria in 1866, and finally France in 1870 – that brought the monarch's liberal opponents to heel and resulted in the political unification of all the German states, *except* for one: Prussia's greatest rival.[5]

Bismarck's so-called *kleindeutsche* ("lesser German") solution – unification *without* Austria – achieved from above what 1848 had not. Almost all of German-speaking Central Europe was finally unified in a single state under a relatively strong central authority, long seen as the antidote to a thousand years of division and discord. But, in the eyes of German liberals, it fell short in other ways. The new German Empire proclaimed in the Hall of Mirrors at Versailles in 1871 was authoritarian to the bone, despite the trappings of democracy. It was one of the first modern European states to adopt universal manhood suffrage, but the new parliament, the Reichstag, had limited powers. Prussia dominated the political system, and conservatives dominated Prussia – as well as the monarchy and the military, the judiciary and the civil service. The emperor appointed the chancellor and decided on almost all matters related to war and peace. The rule of law prevailed, to be sure, but there were no constitutional guarantees of civic freedom similar to the ones enumerated in the 1848 document drafted in Frankfurt.

That did not mean that the Reichstag was completely powerless. It had to approve laws and the budget, including military outlays. This set the stage for frequent showdowns between the chancellor and parliament. Bismarck's preferred strategies for surmounting those disputes were carrots and sticks, divide and rule. In practice, this meant unleashing the powers of the state against alleged "enemies" of the Reich, starting with the persecution of Catholics during the so-called *Kulturkampf* (Cultural Struggle) of the 1870s. It was a paradox, but the "Iron Chancellor" used division to create unity – not for the first or last time in German history.

Turning, say, Bavarian peasants and Ruhr industrialists into "Germans" was one of Bismarck's greatest challenges – and achievements, even if tensions along regional and religious, as well as economic, class, and even ethnic lines remained a core feature of the Kaiserreich. The utter transformation of German society during the last third of the nineteenth century only fueled such divisions. Industrialization and urbanization produced a growing and increasingly well-organized working class, which struck fear in the hearts of those higher up on the social ladder. This made class warfare a mainstay of politics and everyday life – one reason German leaders eventually adopted another strategy aimed at achieving internal consolidation, especially after Bismarck left the political stage in 1890: a more aggressive foreign policy.

Policy differences and personality clashes with the new monarch were the primary cause for his departure. Wilhelm II, whose reign began in 1888, was flamboyant, brash, and mercurial, and his own insecurities seemed to reflect those of German society as a whole. In the decades following unification, the population soared, to be sure, and the country became an industrial behemoth. By the eve of World War I, it had surpassed France and the United Kingdom in most economic metrics, especially the production of goods and materials essential to waging modern warfare, like iron, steel, and chemicals. But despite all this success and achievement, also in the cultural realm, many Germans still felt unsure about their country's "second-class" standing in a world dominated by imperialism. This frequently translated into animosity toward Europe's other major powers.

Those resentments reached new heights in the 1890s, a pivotal decade that witnessed the rise of mass politics in German society – "politics in a new key," in the words of one historian.[6] Mass voting, mass media, and the rise of mass organizations, from trade unions to bellicose ultra-nationalist associations, were all a hallmark of this turbulent era. German leaders and rabid demagogues saw aggressive nationalism as a way to divert attention from challenges at home, as a way to integrate a seemingly divided, heterogeneous nation. They also drew on new, pseudo-biological ideas about racial difference, which found expression in growing contempt for Slavs – and Jews. This period witnessed the rise (and fall) of antisemitic political parties – ironic but not entirely surprising, perhaps, given that *German* Jews were among the most assimilated in all of Europe.

But that was not all. Hoping to secure Germany's "place in the sun," the country abandoned Bismarck's cautious foreign policy following the wars of unification, opting instead for a more confrontational one.[7] In hopes of acquiring more colonies and thus greater international prestige – not to mention raw materials and potential foreign markets for German goods – Wilhelm and his military advisers began a major arms buildup in the late 1890s. This not only led to a costly and volatile naval race with the United Kingdom but also reconfigured the international alliance system – to Germany's distinct disadvantage. The country felt increasingly "encircled" by hostile neighbors. All of these alarming developments set the stage for World War I.

Historians continue to debate whether domestic or foreign considerations were paramount in the minds of German leaders during the July crisis of 1914, triggered (literally) by the assassination of Archduke Franz Ferdinand, the heir to the Habsburg throne. Some argue that Berlin's willingness to go to war was a last-ditch effort to rally the masses to the monarchy and thus defuse worrisome domestic tensions – an "escape forward" (*Flucht nach vorne*) of sorts. They point to Wilhelm's proclamation of a domestic political truce (*Burgfrieden*) at the start of the war: "I no longer recognize political parties," he declared, "I only know Germans."[8]

This latest attempt to overcome internal divisions proved ephemeral. The German left split over whether to support the war; politicians argued over the military's increasingly annexationist aims; extreme material shortages, coupled with four grueling years of brutal trench warfare and stalemate on the Western Front, produced widespread social unrest by 1917. That year, industrial strikes and other forms of protest broke out on the home front. Once it became clear the war was lost, mass discontent erupted in a revolutionary uprising in early November 1918.

The war and its immediate aftermath have since given rise to a number of heated debates. Was Germany mainly responsible, as the victorious nations claimed, for causing that deadly conflagration, in which lethal technological advances allowed for new forms of industrialized killing? Was the November Revolution of 1918, which swept away the monarchy and (ostensibly) the old regime, a failed opportunity to introduce comprehensive reforms that would have ushered in a decisive break from Germany's authoritarian past – yet another turning point in German history that failed to turn? These questions are important because they bear directly on issues that have come to dominate our understanding of – our approach to – modern German history: Why did the country succumb to dictatorship in 1933, and then go on to unleash the deadliest war and most notorious genocide in human history?

Placing the blame squarely on Berlin for the outbreak of World War I justified the harsh terms of the punitive Treaty of Versailles, which forced the defeated country to drastically reduce the size of its military; cede large swathes of territory, including its colonies, to other nations; and make enormous reparations payments to the victors. The treaty's humiliating War Guilt Clause was a lasting source of resentment for Germans across the political spectrum, who blamed the country's new civilian leaders for having accepted it – instead of the military, whose conduct of the war was what had led to defeat in the first place.

The early years of the Weimar Republic were a time of great instability: hyperinflation, political assassinations, armed insurrections by the extreme right and left – including one by an obscure war veteran, Adolf Hitler, who launched a failed "beerhall" putsch in Munich on the fifth anniversary of the November Revolution in 1923. Certain features of the new constitution did not help matters. The adoption of proportional representation for parliamentary elections was laudably democratic but ultimately hindered the formation of stable governing coalitions. Still, the unloved republic enjoyed a half decade of relative stability in the mid- and late 1920s. It shed its pariah status and rejoined the community of nations by promising to make good on its burdensome reparations payments *and* by pledging to solve international disputes without resorting to armed force. Berlin became a global hub of artistic creativity and cultural modernism at the time. Weimar was not "doomed to fail," in short. But then the Great Depression set in – and things fell apart.

Germany was hit worse than most industrial countries, leading to crippling levels of unemployment. Simmering resentment about Versailles, dissatisfaction with the failure of the mainstream political parties to cope effectively with the worsening economic crisis, and a constitutional measure that gave inordinate power to President Paul von Hindenburg, an arch-conservative military hero: all of this paved the way for the collapse of democracy and Hitler's rise to power in late January 1933.

Few subjects have attracted as much popular and scholarly attention as the Third Reich – no surprise, given the central role it played in bringing about the most deadly and destructive war in human history. Hitler's nefarious regime has been the subject of countless debates, many of which touch on essential historical, sociological, and philosophical issues that have meaning beyond the twelve years his "thousand-year empire" actually lasted. These include the ills of modernity and the fragility of democracy; the causes of cowardly collaboration *and* the conditions for heroism in the face of grave danger; humankind's ability to perform unspeakable atrocities.

There are more specific questions about Nazism itself: What was its "essence" – a "form of fascism" or a "brand of totalitarianism"? Did the Third Reich usher in an era of "social reaction" – or a "social revolution" that inadvertently helped modernize German society? Other, more volatile debates have tended to revolve around the figure of the *Führer* himself: Who voted for Hitler and why? Was he a "weak" dictator or a totalitarian autocrat who called all the shots? What role did he ultimately play in the genocide of European Jewry?[9]

Whatever the answers to these challenging questions, one aspect of the Third Reich seems beyond dispute. It was the latest, most radical, and most lethal attempt to establish German hegemony abroad and overcome social divisions at home – and thus provide a lasting, *final* solution to the German Question.

Hitler's notion of a *Volksgemeinschaft* – a racial "people's community" united by "blood" and a "common destiny" – was a new twist on an old concept that Germans had mused about since the late eighteenth century: the achievement of national and ethnic unity across regional, religious, and, later, class divides.

This spoke to a deep-rooted desire for a "harmonic," somehow "organic" social order that would finally eradicate the fractious divisions of the past. Hitler and the Nazis tried to achieve this by creating scapegoats and persecuting pariahs – and, in so doing, wound up unleashing a global war that killed millions; introduced the world to the industrialized mass murder of innocent men, women, and children, simply because of their religion; and, ironically, achieved just the opposite of what they had set out to do. Instead of bringing Germans together, they divided them for decades, in a more impermeable manner than ever before.

1
Defeat (1945–1949)

When the guns of battle fell silent in the spring of 1945, Germany's "total war" had ended in total defeat, and Hitler's "thousand-year empire" lay in ruins. Did that mean that the German Question had finally been resolved? In a way, it had been – in the original sense of the question. At no time were the Germans more united than they were that spring, at least in terms of hunger and hardship, deprivation and desperation, political apathy and impotency. Tens of millions of uprooted Germans and displaced foreigners were on the move; roughly a sixth of the prewar adult population had perished. Aerial warfare had destroyed about a third of all dwellings and a quarter of German industry; the country's infrastructure and transportation system were reduced to rubble. Severe shortages of food and other necessities served as a great equalizer, too, as did the collapse of the Reichsmark, the country's currency since the mid-1920s. This quickly gave rise to a thriving black market, where scarce items were available at exorbitant prices to those who could somehow afford them – resulting in inequities that quickly whittled away any superficial semblance of societal uniformity.

Appearances aside, then, Germans were not all in the same boat. Rural folk were, as a rule, better off than those who lived in urban and industrial areas, which had borne the brunt of British and American bombing raids. Geography mattered, just as it had during the Thirty Years' War of the seventeenth century. Those whose homes and factories had been destroyed, or who had fled or been forced to flee from regions where their families had lived for generations, were much worse off, say, than those who had movable property that could be exchanged on the black market or in the countryside for food and fuel. The arrival of millions of ethnic Germans expelled from the East only exacerbated the burden and increased social fissures by intensifying existing sources of envy and resentment.

Allied policies aimed at "solving" the German Question once and for all further accentuated the differences and divisions. The Big Three (the US, the UK, and the USSR) had already hammered out the broad outlines of those policies at major wartime conferences in Tehran and Yalta, then solidified them shortly after war's end in the imperial city of Potsdam, right outside Berlin. The main goal was to eradicate Nazism from German society and prevent Germany from ever again posing a threat to its neighbors – or itself. Following unconditional surrender, the defeated nation was to be demilitarized, democratized, and "denazified," its economy defanged through far-reaching reform and restructuring. Large swathes of land were taken away, roughly a quarter of Germany's prewar territory. The Allies agreed at Potsdam to the compulsory clearing of ethnic Germans from territory in the East that their ancestors had seized or settled centuries earlier but insisted this be done in an "orderly and humane" fashion.

It was anything *but* for the roughly 12 million individuals who embarked on a traumatic trek westward to escape the advancing Red Army – or were unceremoniously forced from their homes by vengeful Poles and Czechs. These refugees and expellees, primarily women, children, and the elderly, were among those Germans who paid the highest price for the war unleashed by their leaders. Some 2 million perished or went missing along the way, and many of those who made it to the Federal Republic would experience the intense resentment of their new neighbors well into the 1950s.

More punitive, Carthaginian plans to partition and "deindustrialize" the country – and thus turn it into a vast farmland – fell to the wayside when it became clear that that would only undermine efforts to force the Germans to pay for the damage and devastation they had caused. The lessons of Versailles loomed large, and John Maynard Keynes, whose Cassandra-esque warnings about a vindictive settlement had gone unheeded after the last world war, must have felt vindicated.[1] Still, despite the lessons of Versailles and Weimar, the Germans were to pay weighty reparations once again, to the official tune of some $20 billion – half of which was to go to the USSR, which had borne the brunt of destruction. The reparations issue soon created serious divisions among the victorious

Allies themselves, with control of the invaluable Ruhr industrial region in the West proving to be the greatest bone of contention.

Reparations and Reforms, Dismantling and Denazification

Those tensions played a major role in the outbreak of the Cold War, a conflict that would dominate world affairs for the next four decades. In the meantime, Allied policies engendered a great deal of bitterness in Germany itself, which, along with the capital Berlin, was divided for administrative purposes among the Americans, British, French, and Soviets. Rebuffed in the Ruhr, the Soviets took their piece of flesh from their own zone of occupation east of the Elbe, seizing and rigorously removing assorted infrastructure and thousands of factories in recompense for Germany's brutal wartime destruction of the USSR. That "giant sucking sound" in the East prompted some locals to bitterly quip that "our railroad tracks are made of Krupp steel – the Russians' of what they steal."[2]

Industrial dismantling was much less systematic in the three Western zones of occupation, where authorities focused instead on breaking apart banking behemoths, large industrial conglomerates, and infamous chemical combines like IG Farben, which had supplied German death camps in the East with Zyklon B during the war. The Soviets went a step further: they expropriated *and* nationalized, without any compensation, thousands of private firms, both big and small. At the same time, they dismantled large landholdings, especially those of the notorious Junker, the aristocratic landowners in the East who, they believed, were among the main culprits responsible for Nazism.

For all their differences, that was one thing the erstwhile Allies could agree on. Prussian militarism and the Junker, along with other traditional social and economic elites, had lain at the root of Hitler's rise to power and thus had to be eliminated root and branch. Their destruction would solve, once and for all, the German Question – which was why the Allies officially abolished the state of Prussia by decree in February 1947.

These administrative and economic responses to past and potential threats posed by Germany met in the main with sullen resignation. Few were greeted with universal acclaim in the former Reich itself, though the hundreds of thousands in the countryside who benefitted from the Soviet land reform were no doubt grateful for the sudden windfall. There was angry resistance in some circles to educational and administrative reforms intended to change mindsets and mentalities and thus make German society more "democratic," such as the American effort to abolish corporal punishment and the privileged position enjoyed by higher-level civil servants (*Beamte*), another supposed bulwark of German authoritarianism.

But that was just the tip of the iceberg. The millions expelled from the East pined for their lost *Heimat* (homeland), and the brutal sexual abuse of German women, especially though not exclusively in the East, became sources of simmering discontent. Yet nothing seemed to raise the ire of the German populace, at least vocally, as much as the Allies' efforts to root out and punish National Socialists.

That was no easy task, given the high percentage of the population that had belonged to the Nazi Party or one of its many affiliated associations. The Allies arrested tens of thousands of Germans during the months immediately after the war and conducted criminal proceedings against Nazi elites at a series of public trials in the medieval city of Nuremberg. Two dozen prominent figures who had occupied key political, military, and industrial positions during the Third Reich were the focus of the first and most famous trial, which began in November 1945 and lasted almost a year. These "bigwigs" were accused of committing war crimes, crimes against humanity, and wars of aggression – novel legal categories. Other elites – Nazi jurists who had sent political dissidents to their deaths; doctors who had sterilized women, committed euthanasia, or performed "medical" experiments; industrialists who had plundered foreign lands and profited from slave labor – faced the music in a series of subsequent trials, which brought to light the mass crimes perpetrated by and in the name of the German people. Sentences ranged from acquittal to long-term imprisonment to death by hanging.

All four Allies collaborated at the main Nuremberg trial, but after that, they went their separate ways during a second phase that focused on lower-level elites and the "masses." The goal was to determine personal responsibility, identify dyed-in-the-wool ("active") Nazis, and prevent their return to influential positions in public life as judges, teachers, and civil servants. As a rule, the weeding-out process was most far-reaching in the Soviet zone, where occupation authorities carried out a radical purge of the public sector and threw tens of thousands into internment camps – often the same ones the Nazis had previously used to confine their own political foes. Politically reliable "new teachers" and "people's judges" were quickly trained to replace them.

In contrast to efforts in the Soviet zone, the denazification proceedings were largely public in the Western zones, where the accused came before committees composed of fellow Germans who had not incriminated themselves during the Third Reich. Many Germans suffered some form of professional disadvantage, primarily job dismissal, but leniency quickly became the rule of the day. Most escaped with no more than a mild slap on the wrist; they were later "rehabilitated," which meant they could resume their old careers.

There were several reasons for the shift in emphasis toward wrapping up the process quickly and on social and political integration in the new order instead of punishment: the need for technical and professional know-how in the push for German economic recovery, a desire to defuse discontent and forestall political radicalism, as well as a concerted effort to win over Germans as the Cold War heated up. This was especially true as criticism of the entire procedure became increasingly vocal. Those living in the American zone complained about its supposedly unfair or "bureaucratic" nature, as well as its alleged failure to discriminate between "active" and "nominal" Nazis.

Whether denazification was a "failure" or "success" – fair or unjust – remains a topic of heated debate. What is clear is that the political and economic elites of the Third Reich were deprived of power across Germany. At the same time, there was a great deal of personnel continuity at the lower rungs, where many Nazis held on to their positions – also in the eastern half of the country, despite the more radical nature of the Soviet purge. Whatever the flaws and injustices, denazification abruptly came to an end by mid-1948, just as the divisions among the wartime Allies were becoming increasingly palpable – and as the division of Germany itself was quickly becoming a foregone conclusion.

The Road to Division

It cannot be emphasized enough: the separation of Germany into two rival states was neither inevitable nor the original goal of the Allies. Rather, it was the byproduct of increasing tensions and confrontation between the capitalist West and the communist Soviet Union – in a word, of the Cold War. The path to division ran parallel to the division of Europe and eventually much of the world into two opposing blocs. It was true that the Big Three (Roosevelt, Churchill, and Stalin) had decided at Yalta that each would have its own sphere of influence in Germany after victory – and its own zone of occupation in the capital Berlin. But it was also agreed that they would govern the defeated nation jointly and treat it as a single economic unit. The growing gulf over a variety of issues proved insurmountable in the end, with each side blaming the other.

Tracing the steps to division is relatively straightforward, beginning with public disagreements about reparations that broke out at an Allied conference of foreign ministers in Paris in the summer of 1946. Six months later, the Americans and British decided to merge their zones economically into a so-called Bizone. This first concrete step on the path to division came in the face of relentless Soviet – and French – obstruction on the governing Allied Control Council in Berlin, made up of representatives from all four occupying powers and intended as a temporary measure to deal with the economic challenges of occupation. Whatever their differences in outlook and approach, practical considerations remained paramount for all sides, with the Soviets and French placing greater emphasis on reparations and security concerns, the British and Americans on German economic recovery – at a time when the British government was still imposing food and fuel rations on its own citizens.

Was there a point at which division might have been averted? Perhaps, but not after the Western powers decided to introduce a major currency reform in the areas under their control in June 1948. That marked a turning point, and the aftermath of that weighty decision sealed Germany's fate for the next four decades. The currency reform followed on the heels of a major international conference in London that had concluded in June with a recommendation that the Germans living in the West convene an assembly to draw up a constitution for a separate state. The reform itself came in response to the dangers that earlier debt and an unstable currency posed to economic recovery. Its goal was to stimulate economic activity and investment, and it was accompanied by the abolition of price controls on all goods except for essentials like food and rent.

As a result of the currency reform, scarce items became readily available, if at exorbitant prices, and shops filled up literally overnight in the West. This was not yet the famed "economic miracle," but for those Germans living in the West, it was miracle enough. They heartily welcomed this decision – no surprise after having lived under a command economy since the 1930s. Inclusion in the Marshall Plan, or the European Recovery Program (ERP), and thus access to American economic assistance, only sweetened the deal.

The Soviet response could not have been more different. Like the Americans, Stalin was bent on winning the hearts and minds of the Germans. To that end, he played the national card. "Hitlers come and go," he declared during the war, "but Germany and the German people remain."[3] Stalin's goal was a united but neutral Germany, or one solidly in the Soviet camp. That was why devoted German communists in the East mobilized a series of grassroots, pro-unity campaigns aimed at halting division. To no avail.

The currency reform triggered a vigorous response by Moscow, which, in late June 1948, cut off all road and water access to the western sectors of Berlin, which were located deep in Soviet-occupied territory. The goal was to fend off the creation of a new state and drive the Western powers from Berlin by starving its more than 2 million inhabitants into submission. The West responded to this blackmail by sending essential supplies by air to the western sectors. Over the next ten months, American and British cargo planes – "candy bombers" (*Rosinenbomber*) flown by many of the same pilots who, just a few years earlier, had visited death and destruction upon German cities – airlifted approximately 2 million tons of supplies to the more than 2 million Germans living in West Berlin. The operation proceeded like clockwork, with one rescue flight every minute of the day.

In the face of such a determined response, Stalin finally called off the blockade in May 1949, the same month that German representatives completed the Basic Law, a draft constitution for a separate West German state. This was the first but not the last time Moscow would use the former German capital to exert pressure on the West. The blockade, an important turning point in the Cold War *and* on the path to German division, not only failed to achieve Soviet goals but also had an unintended consequence. Politically and psychologically, it signaled a major shift in the relationship between the Western powers and Germans living in the West. The occupants and old foes were now seen as allies and defenders. Without the Cold War and the "freedom fighters" of West Berlin, the West Germans never would have been "rehabilitated" and welcomed into the comity of Western nations so quickly.

The Birth of the Bonn Republic

That shift set the stage for the gradual transfer of greater sovereignty to the Germans. After the war, central political power was vested in the Allied Control Council, whose members acted as custodians of sorts. They made all major political and economic decisions, signed off on significant personnel appointments, and determined which political parties and press organs to permit or prohibit. On May 10, 1949, two days after the German parliamentary body charged with drafting a new constitution had completed its task, the Western powers issued a new Occupation Statute that gave the Germans more control over their own affairs while reserving certain rights and privileges for themselves – over reparations and security issues, for example, control of the Ruhr industrial region, as well as foreign policy and trade.

Eager to restore political life and create structures that would instill democratic ideals, the British, Americans, and French were amenable to ceding so much control, not least because the new constitution fulfilled their basic demands. In almost all respects, the Basic Law was a response to the failings of Weimar and the crimes of National Socialism – and thus an attempt to avoid the fatal errors of yesteryear and solve the German Question from within. Its articles enshrined the rule of law and gave pride of place to the customary catalogue of basic civic freedoms, thus protecting the rights of individuals and minorities. In institutional terms, great emphasis was placed on making the new West German state a representative and not plebiscitary democracy. Power was vested primarily in a governing coalition presided over by a chancellor and responsible to the parliament.

With memories of Paul von Hindenburg's infamous role in the collapse of Weimar democracy, the West German president was given a largely symbolic function as the representative of the state. There were to be no referenda or plebiscites, and a new body, akin to the US Supreme Court, was established to oversee and guarantee the constitutionality of laws and government policies. The Constitutional Court, located in Karlsruhe, marked a major innovation in the German legal tradition.

A strong desire to learn from the mistakes of the recent past found expression in other constitutional measures aimed at preventing a repeat of the chaos, lawlessness, and violence of the interwar period. To prevent the political fragmentation that had made it so difficult to establish stable governing coalitions – and thus paralyzed the Reichstag in the late 1920s and early 1930s – only political parties that received at least 5 percent of the vote would have representation in the new parliament, the Bundestag. In addition, a government could *only* be toppled, in a so-called *constructive* vote of no confidence, if another coalition was agreed upon beforehand. These basic political structures still hold true today. And the main political parties set up at the time – the conservative Christian Democratic Union (CDU) and its Bavarian partner, the Christian Social Union (CSU); the leftist Social Democratic Party (SPD); and the economically liberal Free Democratic Party (FDP), all reconfigurations of the major political parties active before the Nazi "seizure of power" – would dominate the political landscape for the next three decades, until the rise of the environmentalist and pacifist Greens in the late 1970s.

In a move that many non-German westerners would today find surprising and even troubling, the new state adopted strong weapons and took concrete constitutional measures to defend itself against those forces deemed inimical to democracy. This meant, in practice, that individual political parties could be prohibited if the Constitutional Court found them to be undemocratic or a danger to the new republic. That was a controversial measure, but as jurist and politician Carlo Schmid argued at the time, one had to have the courage to be intolerant toward those who wished to use the tools of democracy to destroy it. The Social Democrat had experienced Weimar, its failure, and the consequences of that failure firsthand, and he desperately wished to avoid a repeat performance.[4]

That may have been the most important lesson of Germany's first republic. But it was not the most controversial issue at the time. That distinction fell to a different feature of the new constitution: the relationship between the central government (*Bund*) and the eleven new administrative states (*Länder*). How much power should go to the states was a serious point of contention – no surprise, given German traditions *and* the disastrous effect the consolidation of so much central power had had under the Third Reich. The final decision on the distribution of rights and responsibilities between them (over areas such as education, for example) did not fully satisfy either camp: those who preferred a strong central government, and those who, like the French, favored a more confederal system.

The creation of a second legislative chamber that represented the interests of the states was seen as a compromise. But even more important than that body, the Bundesrat, was the conviction that all this would only be temporary. The preamble and articles of the Basic Law, which called for, foresaw, and oversaw the modalities of German unity at one point in the not-too-distant future, underscored the very belief in the transitory nature of the new West German state. The German Question was deferred for the moment but clearly remained on the table.

Stalin's Unloved Stepchild

If the Federal Republic of Germany was a "child" of the Cold War, the German Democratic Republic was Stalin's "unwanted" or "unloved" stepchild.[5] The Soviet leader eventually realized that a united but neutral or Soviet-style Germany was not in the immediate cards and grudgingly signed off on the creation of a separate East German state in late 1948 – but only after a West German one was established. That was why the Soviet zone seemed to be playing catch-up, but this was by design: it placed the onus of division on the West. Three weeks after the formation of the first West German government in mid-September 1949, the East German parliament, the People's Chamber (*Volkskammer*), convened for the first time on October 7, the day the GDR was officially established. One of its first acts was to adopt a new constitution, a document that had all the trappings of democracy in the tradition of 1848 and Weimar. But that was deceptive.

The similarities between the two new constitutions were as striking as the differences. Like the Basic Law, the East German version enshrined the traditional catalogue of basic civil rights and liberties for all its citizens. In both instances, this was an unmistakable statement about – and rejection of – the atrocities committed by the state against the individual under the Third Reich. But there were not-so-subtle differences as well. The East German constitution took with one hand what it gave with the other. In the same breath it guaranteed equality before the law, it criminalized a wide range of activities imprecisely described as "rabblerousing." This was, on the face of it, another rebuff to the crimes of the recent past. But in practice, officials would make arbitrary use of this provision to quash dissent and behavior deemed somehow inimical to the new state.

Would it be misleading to draw a parallel here to the West German constitution's efforts to defend the state against political foes? East German officials would use the provisions of its constitution against *individuals* and in an incomparably more indiscriminate manner. There were nevertheless similarities. Both documents reflected a keen desire to protect and defend the two newly created states against (real or imagined) foes from within and without and were thus products of Cold War hysteria. But that was not all. They also bore witness to the trauma of Weimar and the Third Reich.

To that extent, and in not entirely dissimilar ways, the two constitutions represented real efforts, at least on paper, to "come to terms" with the recent past. This was not the type of *Vergangenheitsbewältigung* that later became familiar in West Germany, beginning in the late 1960s and 1970s. But at a time when procuring enough food and fuel was the paramount concern of most Germans, dealing with *that* aspect of the past – the criminal barbarity of the regime, especially toward the Jews – was not on many minds. The focus instead was on their own suffering.

That was especially true in the GDR, whose leaders felt little sense of responsibility for the horrors of the Third Reich. After all, most of them had sat in prison or gone into exile in the 1930s and 1940s. Besides, they claimed, most Nazis had magically absconded to the West after the war. The disturbing irony was that the East German state would become nearly as repressive at home – though by no means as murderous – as the Nazi regime, and the groundwork for that was already being laid in the second half of the 1940s. German communist leaders who had spent the Third Reich in exile in the USSR returned home in the spring of 1945, and the party program they published that June assiduously avoided any reference to communism, socialism, or radical reform. This progressive but moderate document deceptively called instead for a parliamentary democracy and came out in favor of private property and free trade.

With an eye to the internecine fighting on the Left that had helped paved the way for the Nazi "seizure of power," communist leaders initially made overtures to the Social Democrats in the hope of unifying the working classes. But, backed by Soviet occupation forces and fearing that they would lose a free and open election, they dropped all pretenses within a year and forced a merger with the SPD in April 1946. Staunch anticommunist sentiment on the part of Social Democrats living in the Western zones meant that the merger only took place in the East. An iconic handshake between two leaders of the KPD (*Kommunistische Partei Deutschlands*) and SPD marked the establishment of the new Socialist Unity Party (*Sozialistische Einheitspartei Deutschlands*, SED), a shotgun marriage that sealed the division from the Social Democrats in the West. That was when the gloves came off.

Those Social Democrats who were critical of the merger and proved uncooperative soon wound up in prison – often in the same concentration camps set up by the Nazis in the 1930s, like Buchenwald. Political repression quickly extended to other groups as the Cold War heated up, and the focus shifted from weeding out Nazis to eliminating any and all political foes. Soviet authorities permitted the establishment of parties that represented the middle classes and farmers, but they were quickly tamed. When their leaders voiced criticism of sacrosanct policies and developments, they, too, were subject to persecution. Those not imprisoned either caved to the pressure or fled to the West, leading to the establishment of separate parties with similar names and constituencies in the East and West. This only reinforced the process of division.

The SED was hailed as a "party of a new type," a Marxist–Leninist "cadre party" that hewed closely to the Stalinist model of "democratic socialism." This meant, in theory if not necessarily practice, complete control by central authorities, absolute party discipline, and utter subjugation to Moscow. The occupation officially ended with the founding of the GDR in October 1949, but East German officials slavishly continued to follow the directives of Soviet authorities, who kept close tabs on all developments and reserved the right to intervene in domestic affairs. Moscow dictated East German foreign policy, as well as the general direction of all major decisions at home. This undermined any semblance of legitimacy for the new regime, which one scholar dismissively stamped a Soviet "satrapy."[6] As in ancient times, the East German one would nevertheless enjoy considerable autonomy in its day-to-day rule.

In short, the new East German state was an authoritarian dictatorship devoid of democratic legitimacy. In contrast to the West, there was no separation of powers, no independent judiciary, and no federal form of government. All power was concentrated in the hands of the SED and central authorities. Elections were a sham, thanks to predetermined lists of candidates that assured the ascendancy of the SED and its affiliate organizations. Crude censorship of the media and political indoctrination in the schools further shored up communist domination, as did the filling of key positions with loyal communist cadres: in the government, judiciary, and bureaucracy, in the police and local administrative apparatuses, in the schools and universities.

Educational reform was more far-reaching in the Soviet zone, where a fundamental shake-up of seemingly "reactionary" educational structures, practices, and personnel took place. But it was by no means "democratic." Yes, the children of industrial laborers, farmers, and other traditionally disadvantaged socio-economic groups gained greater and even privileged access to higher-level learning. But instruction was patently politicized and irritatingly ideological, and students were force-fed a crude Marxist catechism – ironic, of course, in a place where traditional religion was no longer taught in the schools.

German–German Parallels

There were palpable differences between the two halves of postwar Germany by the end of the decade: a federal, democratic political system and free-market, capitalist economy in the West, where prewar elites and institutional traditions proved surprisingly resilient; an autocratic, one-party dictatorship presiding over a command economy in the East, where the traditional social hierarchy had been turned upside down.

Yet, for all their differences, there were notable similarities and parallels. Each state belonged to – and eventually came to represent, in the heart of Europe – one of two rival blocs characterized by opposing political, social, and economic systems. By no means were they equal members of these new alliances born of the Cold War, and that was something else they had in common. Each had to accept palpable limits on its sovereignty, as well as continuing occupation by foreign forces – even if the exact nature of these constraints differed considerably in the East and West. In short, Germans in both states had to pay the cost of the war and confront the consequences that flowed from military defeat: a far-ranging political and administrative purge and other assorted measures intended to exorcise any residual fascist demons.

There were other commonalities. Militarism and the aristocracy had been discredited in both states, each of which experienced a political rebirth of sorts by decree, marked by the rapid emergence of a stable party landscape – more by design than by choice in the East. The two new states also faced similar challenges early on. Each had to provide for and integrate millions of disgruntled refugees from the East while clawing its way out of the rubble to rebuild, both literally and figuratively.

Women played a major role in those efforts on both sides of the Elbe. The absence and eventual death of millions of men who had gone off to fight in the steppes and tundra of the Soviet Union or the deserts of North Africa meant that women were forced to assume new responsibilities during and after the war. The need to provide for one's family increasingly fell on their shoulders, which was why so many entered – and, in the East, would remain in – the workforce. The so-called rubble women (*Trümmerfrauen*) who helped dig Germany out from under all the destruction became, like the black market and the use of cigarettes as a form of currency, a lasting symbol of the immediate postwar period. Just as important, they underscored the partial reversal of traditional gender roles, even if the image of women cleaning up the mess their men had made was nothing new.

The West Germans had an easier job of it, of course. They quickly became the recipients of generous economic assistance, whereas the East Germans suffered under severe Soviet economic exploitation and political repression. That did not mean that anger and resentment were limited to only one half of the now divided country. Industrial strikes and hunger protests in the West punctuated discontent about material shortages and fresh forms of socioeconomic inequality. Unpopular policies like denazification and educational reform were important sources of irritation as well.

But the Americans, British, and French were careful not to push too far – again, one of the ways in which the Cold War accrued to the benefit of ordinary Germans. And that was why, by the close of the decade, the Western allies had gradually won the support and allegiance – the hearts and minds – of those living under their control. In the East, by contrast, the Soviets and their German lackeys remained largely unpopular, which was why they felt compelled to rely on brute force to quell any potential unrest from below. A humanitarian airlift in the West – the threat of imprisonment in the East: the contrast could not have been starker.

2
Revival (1949–1961)

With commendable confidence and, it turns out, great foresight, Swiss journalist Fritz René Allemann declared in a widely read book from 1956 that "Bonn [was] not Weimar."[1] That reassuring catchphrase quickly became synonymous with the stability of the Federal Republic, whose leaders had established the new seat of government in Bonn, a quaint university town on the Rhine River far from both Berlin, the old imperial capital, and the town where the Weimar constitution had been drafted in 1919. Both cities now lay far beyond the Iron Curtain.

There were no comparable claims in the West about East Germany. Politics aside, there was good reason for that. The GDR's viability seemed much less certain at the time, just three years after a statewide, popular uprising that had to be put down with Soviet tanks. The communist regime would nevertheless endure for another three decades, longer than the Weimar Republic and the Third Reich combined. For vastly different reasons, Pankow – the drab district in East Berlin that served as the seat of the new socialist government – was not Weimar, either. The 1950s was essentially the story of how *both* states became both permanent and stable, and it was their very stability that provided a working solution to the German Question – at least for the time being, and at the cost of national unity.

"Economic Miracles" and the "Social Market Economy"

If there were a hierarchy of reasons for the stability – *and* political volatility – of the two German states, economic performance would be at or near the top. Let's begin with West Germany. By the time the infamous Berlin Wall was built in the summer of 1961, the Federal Republic had enjoyed more than a decade of sustained economic growth and unprecedented prosperity. Full employment, stable prices, rising real wages and salaries, new export records: the figures spoke for themselves, especially in the economy's most important sector, industry. Observers began to speak of an "economic miracle."

That was a misnomer. Miracles cannot be explained, and the *Wirtschaftswunder* certainly could. Marshall Plan aid and the currency reform of 1948 provided a jumpstart. The Korean War, demand for Germany's famed industrial products, and a new international system dedicated to free trade all allowed for a boom in exports in a world where, despite Hitler and what later became known as the Holocaust, "Made in Germany" still enjoyed great cachet. Just as essential were pent-up consumer desires at home following the "hunger years" of the 1940s. The West Germans profited, too, from the confidence that came from knowing that the country had the backing and protection of the United States, the world's wealthiest and strongest superpower.

There is another factor worth mentioning. Many of the challenges faced early on proved beneficial in the long term. Refugees from the East, once integrated, helped replenish the ranks of a labor force decimated by total warfare. Just as important, new infrastructure and more modern factories eventually came to replace the old and often obsolete ones destroyed during the war. This was why many foreigners would later grumble – with an eye to Germany *and* Japan – that the military losers of the war had become the economic victors of the peace.

The upswing was not just limited to the Federal Republic. But it confirmed the merits of the "social market economy" advocated so energetically by the West German minister of economics, Ludwig Erhard. This paradoxical term described an economic system that allowed for the relatively unbridled play of market forces, free trade, and competition. At the same time, it protected individuals against excessive exploitation while ensuring them a certain degree of economic and social security. It was a system, in other words, where the state promoted economic freedom and the pursuit of profit while guaranteeing social justice and responsibility.

Promising "prosperity for all," as the title of a bestseller by Erhard put it – and building on German traditions going back to the late nineteenth century – the Federal Republic adopted an array of programs aimed at providing its citizens with more than just a modicum of social protection.[2] The initial focus was on those *Germans* who had suffered most physically and materially because of the war: refugees, disabled soldiers, the widows and children of fallen soldiers, those who had lost their homes – roughly a third of the population. The most important measure here was the 1952 Equalization of Burdens Law (*Lastenausgleichsgesetz*), which introduced a supplementary income tax that led to the largest transfer of funds in German history up to that point. A similar attempt to compensate those who had endured great hardship because of the war, primarily by those who had remained relatively unscathed, would be adopted following unification in 1990.

Other significant social welfare measures included massive investment in new housing projects, leading to the construction of more than 5 million apartments in the 1950s alone; the disbursement of *Kindergeld* ("child support money"), a practice first begun during the Third Reich; and, most controversially, the passing in 1957 of a novel reform that tied pension levels to the earnings of those still active in the workforce. The reform lifted millions of pensioners out of poverty, and, for the first time in German history, the elderly now received adequate levels of state support – in stunning contrast to the GDR, where pensions were woefully inadequate.

Economic Struggles and Insurrection in the East

It was West Germany's astonishing economic success that allowed for such largesse. Social and material inequality did not disappear, but even the poorest came to expect a higher standard of living than ever before, and that made such inequalities more bearable. The pie was indeed getting bigger, as Erhard had promised, along with each slice.

The situation was much different in East Germany, even though the regime's material aspirations were just as ambitious. The GDR's vaunted social welfare benefits included subsidized foodstuffs, low-cost housing, cheap transportation, free childcare, as well as a variety of public and workplace facilities designed to lighten the load of working men and women. But the lackluster performance of the command economy, which slavishly followed the Soviet example, made it extremely difficult for the regime to satisfy demand and make good on its promises. As a result, severe shortages of even the most basic foodstuffs, consumer durables, housing, and kindergarten spots were frustratingly common throughout the 1950s and beyond. Access to items in short supply typically involved long waits queuing in front of state-owned stores, or reliance on personal connections that often involved barter.

Both states faced similar challenges at the outset: wartime destruction, a ruined infrastructure, severe shortages of housing and basic consumer goods, hunger, unemployment, and poverty, all made worse by the need to care for and integrate millions of returning soldiers, evacuees, and uprooted refugees from the East. So, what accounted for the comparatively poor showing of the East German economy? Was it doomed from the outset, or because of later policy decisions?

For one, the Federal Republic enjoyed a more advantageous starting point, having escaped both the extreme plundering visited by the Soviets upon the Eastern zone, as well as the overzealous nationalization of key industries. It also had a much larger population. A lack of natural resources and the disruption of prewar trading relations and markets in the West that could absorb East German products also played a role. Equally important were bureaucratic ineptitude and rigid centralized planning; the absence of self-correcting market mechanisms and the gradual elimination of private business and manufacturing; investment in "heavy industry" (coal and steel) instead of consumer goods; and the loss of almost 3 million people who – for personal, political, or economic reasons – fled to the Federal Republic from 1950 to 1961 alone. In contrast to the West Germans, who could count on the wealthy United States for trade and economic support, the East Germans hitched their wagon to an exhausted USSR bent on exacting reparations and improving its own economic well-being at the cost of its allies in Eastern Europe.

All was not dismal. The GDR did inherit highly developed enterprises in major sectors like chemicals and optics and, like West Germany, it enjoyed huge gains in industrial output and gross domestic product (GDP) in the 1950s. But this did not raise consumption levels and living conditions to ones on par with those of the Federal Republic. Economic planning proved to be highly inefficient, even though, at great human cost, it had so successfully turned the Soviet Union into a major industrial power in the 1930s. Because of the single-minded, Stalinist focus on *quantitative* output and not quality, a series of multiyear economic "plans" hammered out and enforced by officials on high failed to achieve their goals and satisfy consumer demand. The ruling communist party failed to solve, in short, a major dilemma of its own making: how to boost economic efficiency without relinquishing central control of the micromanaged economy.

All of this would lead to the uprising of June 17, 1953, the greatest threat to East German authorities prior to the fall of 1989. On that day, hundreds of thousands of East Germans forcibly took to the streets to protest against the regime. Initiated by angry construction workers in Berlin three months after Stalin's death, the first state-wide insurrection in the Soviet bloc was set off by a series of recently adopted but highly unpopular policies, all part of a rash attempt to rapidly "construct socialism." These measures included a palpable increase in state repression, the beginning of forced agricultural collectivization, and, most fatefully, an across-the-board hike in production quotas for workers.

Acting on orders from Moscow, which recognized the volatility of the situation, East German authorities had already announced a "New Course" in early June. All the unpopular measures were rescinded – *except* for the one specifically affecting the manual laborers in whose name the party claimed to rule. It was that omission that ignited the revolt. Disgruntled East Germans from almost all regions and social groups joined the protest, which initially focused on socioeconomic issues but quickly turned to political ones as well, with calls for free elections and an end to one-party rule. The demonstrations could only be quelled with the forceful assistance of Soviet tanks and occupation troops, which attested to the embryonic state of the East German security apparatus at that time – even though the infamous Ministry for State Security, or Stasi, had doubled in size over the course of 1952 alone. It also made clear that the regime's very existence was only guaranteed by the hundreds of thousands of Soviet soldiers stationed on East German soil.

The SED weathered the storm, but the New Course did not lead to long-term fundamental changes – a point later driven home by the dismal disappointment of the Seven-Year Plan of 1959, which vowed with great hubris that per capita consumption and worker productivity in the GDR would surpass that of the

Federal Republic by the mid-1960s. Instead, quality, innovation, and productivity remained poor, persistently outstripped in the West. The supply situation improved to some extent, but a modernization campaign, a "scientific-technological revolution" proclaimed with great fanfare in the late 1950s, did not bear any real fruit until the following decade – and even then, the results were modest. There was an undeniable parallel here to developments in the Federal Republic, where the iconic images of overflowing shop windows immediately following the currency reform of 1948 misleadingly suggested a sudden affluence that didn't really materialize until the late 1950s and especially the 1960s.[3]

Leisurely "Americanization" and Slavish "Sovietization"

The Federal Republic's founding decade nevertheless witnessed an unmistakable rise in the living standards of most West Germans, as real wages increased, on average, more than 5 percent annually. This allowed for greater and more demonstrative consumption practices that helped put the deprivations of the 1940s behind them. A so-called *Freßwelle* ("eating frenzy") in the early 1950s was followed by a *Reisewelle*, or "traveling craze" – especially to warmer climes abroad like Italy and Spain – made possible by the spread of mass tourism and a fourfold increase in car ownership that decade. The five millionth Volkswagen Beetle, *the* symbol of the "economic miracle," rolled off the assembly line just months after the mortar holding the Berlin Wall together had hardened.

A more intense pursuit of leisure activities and increasingly homogeneous purchasing habits were another hallmark of this new "consumer society," thanks to higher disposable incomes, the gradual introduction of a shorter, five-day workweek, an increase in vacation days (another practice begun under the Nazis), as well as the advent of time-saving household appliances and other consumer durables. Radio and cinema remained popular, and television was in its infancy, but the latter was well on its way to becoming the preferred pastime of many West Germans by the late 1950s.

All of this contributed to the growing "Americanization" of West German society in terms of tastes, lifestyles, outlooks, and sensibilities. Most obvious was the influence of Hollywood, jazz, and rock-and-roll. The reaction was ambivalent, just as it had been since the interwar period: admiration and enthusiasm, especially by youths; wariness, condescension, and even resentment on the part of their elders. The fervor for jazz, for example, provoked the same type of racist criticism common before the war, and this was true on both sides of the Iron Curtain. As the cultural expression of downtrodden "negroes," blues music eventually enjoyed the grudging approval of East German ideologues. But all things American, from jeans to rock-and-roll, remained highly suspicious to authorities in the GDR, where many young people, like their counterparts in the West, eagerly embraced these "subversive imperialist exports."[4]

The counterpart to creeping Americanization in the Federal Republic was formal Sovietization in the East in the political, economic, and cultural realms. But there was a major difference. Few became convinced by the catchy slogan, "To learn from the Soviet Union means to learn victory." Whatever the feelings of ambivalence toward the United States, most West Germans responded positively, even enthusiastically, to "Westernization," especially given the alternative. For their part, most ordinary East Germans remained hostile to, or at least highly skeptical of, "Sovietization" in its various guises: repressive, one-party rule; a command economy obsessed with heavy industry; censorship and conformity to the dour, didactic tenets of "socialist realism," an uninspired, highly literal artistic style that idealized life under state socialism. No matter. Armed with Marx's and Lenin's teachings about historical inevitability and "scientific socialism," East German leaders remained convinced that they were on the proper path to a glorious future.

Stability through Social Integration

Increased consumption and leisure, as well as generous social welfare policies, were so important because they contributed to the stability of the new West German state, largely by accomplishing what the Weimar Republic – and the GDR – had failed to do: win the hearts and minds of the populace and thus integrate persons who posed a potential threat to domestic stability. The West German Equalization of Burdens Law, an impressive act of mutual solidarity, defused the potential for radicalization on the part of the millions of refugees from the East, who would become more accepted by and more accepting of their new *Heimat* by the 1960s. Their eventual integration was one of the young republic's most impressive achievements.

Different policies helped appease the disgruntled in East Germany, who gradually but much less enthusiastically came to terms with the new regime. Refugees there, for example, received confiscated landholdings during the land reform of the late 1940s – a popular measure, even if many of these "new farmers" later failed or lost their holdings during the collectivization campaigns of the 1950s. The distribution of coveted privileges – access to scarce goods like adequate housing, the opportunity to study at university or receive a promotion – to groups and individuals deemed most essential to East German society, for political, economic, and ideological reasons, was another way to secure allegiance. At the same time, it alienated those who did not enjoy such benefits. This posed a potential source of instability and was indeed a driving force behind the mass uprising of June 1953. In any event, the regime was especially committed to offering material "blandishments" to industrial workers, especially following that upheaval, which would long haunt East German leaders.

In both states, the reintegration of former Nazis was equally essential for promoting stability. Thanks to a series of West German amnesty laws, most were legally "rehabilitated" and allowed to return to their old positions and professions by the early 1950s, even in the judiciary and foreign office. One of the most egregious cases was that of Hans Globke, a jurist who had helped write the legal commentary on the anti-semitic Nuremberg Laws of 1935 – and later became one of the most trusted advisers of Konrad Adenauer, West Germany's first chancellor. But even in the GDR, where a more stringent denazification took place, authorities willfully ignored the past of many who had incriminated themselves during the Third Reich *if* they embraced the new regime (at least ostensibly). Besides, that and other skeletons in the closet could later be used to ensure obedience.

The fact that thousands of Nazi elites and even mass murderers received no more than a slap on the wrist was morally reprehensible. One might well wonder how West Germany managed to become a functioning and stable democracy despite this failure. But the converse also makes sense. The willingness to turn a blind eye to past crimes and give the incriminated a chance to rejoin society as "upstanding citizens" was precisely what underpinned the political permanence of the West German state. It was, in a sense, the price for stability – and that had priority in the new Cold War atmosphere, which made it easier for the former wartime Allies to turn a blind eye to the past. New enemies replaced the ones of yesteryear. As a result, a more open confrontation with the past would only really begin the following decade, in the 1960s.

Most former Nazis managed to conform and remain inconspicuous, and many even became "good" democrats whose (nonlethal) skills and expertise were a benefit to the rest of society. The lethal skills of others were a benefit to the two new superpowers – like those of émigré Wernher von Braun, who developed the V2 rocket for Hitler during World War II and later helped the United States put the first person on the moon. The unrepentant joined neo-Nazi groups and organizations, including the Socialist Reich Party (*Sozialistische Reichspartei Deutschlands*, SRP) and the German Reich Party (*Deutsche Reichspartei*, DRP). The state came down hard on these individuals and groupings – the new Constitutional Court even banned the SRP in 1952 – and, as a result, the radical right performed poorly at the polls, receiving less than 1 percent of the vote in federal elections that year. In 1956, the KPD suffered the same fate as the SRP, after years of persecution by state authorities redolent of the McCarthy era in the United States – *and* of the concurrent East German campaign against "cosmopolitans," that is, Jewish communist functionaries arrested and purged from the SED for supposedly serving as "agents" of "global Zionism."[5]

Parallel Political Developments

The Social Democrats were not banned in West Germany, but they were more or less sidelined in the Federal Republic in the 1950s – as they had been in the GDR following the forced fusion of the Socialist Unity Party in 1946. There were other parallels between the party landscapes of the two postwar German states, though, as in the case of the SPD, for much different reasons. Both were dominated by a single party: the conservative CDU in the West, the communist SED in the East. The former had managed to achieve that position by the force of its program and policies, the latter by force alone. At the time of the first federal election in 1949, there were more than a dozen political parties in the Federal Republic. The smaller ones had more or less vanished by the end of the following decade thanks to constitutional safeguards *and* to the CDU's popular domestic and foreign policies. These gradually weaned voters away from parties with more specialized constituencies, like those that represented the interests of former refugees from the East.

By the late 1950s, then, if for strikingly different reasons, smaller parties had become politically insignificant in both states – a development that contributed, in much different ways, to the very *stability* of those states. This was inextricably linked in the West to Konrad Adenauer, the septuagenarian Rhinelander who led the CDU and became the first chancellor of the Federal Republic in September 1949. After winning a bitterly fought campaign against the SPD under the leadership of Kurt Schumacher, who had spent much of the Third Reich in various concentration camps, Adenauer went on to head the West German government until 1963: a longer period than all of the almost two dozen Weimar cabinets put together.

At the time, few would have predicted such longevity, political or otherwise. Almost the same age that Otto von Bismarck had been when the Iron Chancellor *left* office, Adenauer was not a well-known figure at the end of the war. A middle-class politician and former mayor of Cologne, he became chairman of the CDU in the British zone of occupation in 1946 and then served as president of the assembly that drafted the Basic Law three years later.

The system of government created by that document has often been described as a *Kanzlerdemokratie* ("chancellor democracy"), a designation that highlights the considerable powers the West German constitution bestows upon the office of chancellor. It is he or she who appoints and dismisses cabinet ministers, he or she who alone determines and assumes responsibility for government policy. But it was Adenauer's personal governing style that first gave the term its true meaning. Thanks to his great political gifts, pragmatism, and cunning, he completely dominated the West German political stage during his tenure. His calm Rhenish disposition and disarming sense of humor helped disguise the unscrupulous political methods he occasionally used to achieve his goals; at the same time, his ability to explain complex issues in relatively simple (and sometimes simplistic) terms made him an avuncular figure who inspired trust and confidence. During the long 1950s, the patriarchal Adenauer personified the Federal Republic at home and abroad.

Walter Ulbricht, Adenauer's communist counterpart, had a similar political standing in the GDR, where he was the dominant – and domineering – figure. But that was where the similarities ended. Born into a working-class milieu in the Saxon city of Leipzig in 1893, the trained cabinetmaker joined the KPD soon after its founding in 1919 and rapidly ascended its ranks during the Weimar period. He went into exile after the Nazis came to power and spent the war years in the Soviet Union, returning to Germany in 1945 to help re-establish the KPD. Ulbricht oversaw the creation of the SED a year later, and as its General Secretary (later First Secretary), he quickly became the most powerful political figure in the GDR, weathering and emerging even stronger from the storm of June 1953.

Western Integration, Eastern Integration

Adenauer and Ulbricht were the main domestic driving forces behind the political, economic, and military integration of the two Germanies into each of the opposing Cold War camps – a process as important for their stability as the social, political, and economic integration of the potentially disaffected. Tensions nevertheless remained pronounced in both states between a lingering wish for national unity and a strong desire to re-enter the community of nations as equal and sovereign members. This issue was *the* Gordian knot of the 1950s. Adenauer's priority was clearly the latter, but that did not mean he was opposed in principle to unification on terms favorable to the Federal Republic, or that he purposefully sabotaged *genuine* chances to bring it about.

The best known "missed opportunity" was the series of so-called Stalin Notes of 1952, in which the Soviet dictator offered the prospect of German unity in return for strict neutrality. The Western powers, joined by the Bonn government, dismissed the proposals as an insincere, cynical maneuver intended to forestall plans to rearm the Federal Republic and integrate it militarily into the Western alliance – which is surely what they were.[6] Moscow had long been calling for a single German state, to be sure, and a steady stream of appeals for unity had flowed from the East, beginning with the so-called "People's Congress" movement of the late 1940s. SED leaders were extremely chary of unity, in fact, even as they swore an unwavering commitment to achieving it. After all, chances were high it would result in their fall from power.

Whatever the actual commitment to national unification on the part of their leaders, both states moved further and further away from each other, a product and expression of the growing conflict between the two superpowers. Their inexorable integration into the two rival Cold War blocs went hand in hand with the gradual recovery of sovereignty over the course of the 1950s. The latter was more formal than real in the case of the GDR, and, in practice, the international constellation continued to limit both states' room for maneuver, both domestically and in terms of their foreign policy. Trying to secure more was something they also had in common.

A series of international agreements in 1955 abrogated the Occupation Statute of 1949 (see p. 33) and thus marked West Germany's formal acquisition of sovereignty, even if the new state had already been well on its way to becoming more of a subject than a mere object in the international arena. The first major steps in this direction, and on the path to West European integration, were safeguards intended to allay the fears of the Federal Republic's neighbors, whose memories of German nationalism, military aggression, and formidable economic strength remained fresh. This included memberships in the Organisation for European Economic Co-operation (OEEC) in 1949, which oversaw the distribution of Marshall Plan aid, and then in the European Coal and Steel Community (ECSC) in 1952.

Initiated by the French, the ECSC placed under the control of an international authority the production of these two commodities so essential for industrial and military might. In so doing, this supranational institution gave the Federal Republic a more equal standing vis-à-vis the other major West European states, whose economic sovereignty was now similarly restricted. The signing of the Treaty of Rome five years later created the European Economic Community (EEC), an international organization aimed at increasing economic cooperation and reducing trade barriers among the member states. This marked the crowning moment of West Germany's incorporation into the Western alliance as an (almost) equal partner.

The GDR continued to play a game of catch-up that decade – without ever catching up in the areas that truly mattered: popular support, political legitimacy, and economic success. It joined the Council for Mutual Economic Assistance (Comecon), a Soviet and East European trading bloc, in September 1950, less than a year after the Federal Republic had joined the OEEC, and it became a founding member of the Warsaw Pact less than two weeks after West Germany had gained sovereignty and joined the North Atlantic Treaty Organization (NATO) in early May 1955. The GDR was granted formal sovereignty itself just a few months later in September. Its leaders nevertheless remained subservient to Moscow, even if they habitually worried the Kremlin might abandon them by striking some sort of disadvantageous deal with the West. Wary politicians in Bonn harbored similar concerns about Washington, London, and Paris – fears of "Rapallo" in reverse, so to speak.[7]

Nikita Khrushchev, the new Soviet strongman following Stalin's death in March 1953, allayed such fears in the East when he proclaimed in 1955 that unification was an issue to be determined by the Germans themselves – only to create new concerns the following year with his "destalinization" campaign, which disquieted East German leaders because of its destabilizing effects. Unrest in Poland and Hungary in the wake of Khrushchev's "Secret Speech" of February 1956, which exposed Stalin's crimes and ushered in a political and cultural "thaw," confirmed such fears. But the Soviet Union did not seriously plan on abandoning the GDR, not least because its economy had already become the most productive in Eastern Europe – *despite* the many disadvantages of membership in the Comecon, where economic benefits (unlike those of the EEC) accrued primarily to a single state, the USSR.

Moscow's steadfast commitment to its German ally became even more pronounced with the beginning of a new crisis in the winter of 1958. Increasingly alarmed about the sustained exodus of East Germans via West Berlin – not just a Cold War battleground and hotbed of espionage but also an enticing enclave, a magnetic "showcase" of Western prosperity and political freedom (propped up by massive subsidies from Bonn) – Khrushchev threatened that November to unilaterally alter the postwar status of the former German capital and turn it into a demilitarized "free city." Whenever he wished to make the West scream, Khrushchev later commented, he would "squeeze" Berlin, the "testicles of the West."[8] East Germans

– faced with the very real possibility that the most popular exit route to the West was about to be cut off – now swarmed to the wealthy Federal Republic in unprecedented numbers, swelled further by a fresh collectivization drive in the countryside and a new campaign calling for repressive "class struggle."

Soviet and East German officials responded to this massive flight by adopting an extraordinary measure that grabbed international headlines in August 1961: the construction of a twelve-foot-high, ninety-six-mile-long concrete and barbed wire barrier that hermetically sealed off West Berlin from the GDR. This effectively stanched the destabilizing flow of labor and talent to the West – nearly 50,000 East Germans fled during the first two weeks of August 1961 alone – and put the final touch, literally and figuratively, on German division. In so doing, the Wall became the most iconic symbol of the Cold War. For Germans themselves, that infamous *lieu de mémoire* embodied – like no other located in Germany itself – the tragedy of their country's most recent history.[9]

Societal Parallels

The German Question remained at the heart of the Cold War in the long 1950s. At the same time, *the* defining international conflict of the postwar era made it a less pressing issue, especially after the construction of the Wall. But more than anything else, the Cold War (coupled with traumatic memories of

Versailles) allowed for the rapid rehabilitation and integration of the two German states into the two rival blocs, making it both a blessing *and* a curse. That was also why their new partners and overlords – some enthusiastically, some grudgingly – were willing to put the recent past behind them and even countenance German rearmament, especially following the outbreak of war on the similarly divided Korean peninsula in 1950.

West Germany was allowed to create an army and join NATO in 1955, following the failure to create a so-called European Defense Community, a French initiative aborted in the end by the French themselves, who felt threatened by the prospect of any German rearmament. To allay such fears, the Federal Republic formally pledged not to produce atomic, biological, or chemical weapons. The creation of a West German military and the stationing of atomic weapons on German soil nevertheless unleashed a torrent of protest *at home* by a broad coalition that included the churches and youths, the SPD and the unions, scientists and intellectuals. This culminated in the Göttingen Manifesto of 1957, signed by eighteen prominent German physicists opposed to arming the new Bundeswehr with tactical nuclear weapons.[10] In agreeing to remilitarization in return for greater sovereignty, Adenauer went against the wishes of the majority – just as he had within his own party, when members of the CDU opposed the Luxemburg Agreements of 1952, a deal the chancellor had reached with Israel to pay compensation to Holocaust survivors.

The protest movement failed to achieve its goals, but it did offer a foretaste of what would come a decade later during the Vietnam era. Just as important, it attested to an important evolution in the German mentality. The trauma of World War II, coupled with the strong likelihood that the next military conflict would be fought against *other* Germans just across the Elbe, had gone a long way in exorcising any residual militarist demons.

There was no organized protest against growing militarization in the GDR, but many ordinary East Germans harbored similar feelings. Anger about the diversion of essential resources toward the military was, in fact, one of the main grievances voiced during the June 1953 upheaval. Authorities were especially worried about those men who steadfastly refused to join the various paramilitary organizations created in the 1950s to defend the new state against enemies, both foreign and domestic. Youths were particularly resistant to the massive enlistment campaigns that decade, especially following the creation of the National People's Army in 1956. Many expressed pacifist sentiments similar to their counterparts in the Federal Republic.

That's important because it alerts us to some striking if unexpected parallels between societal and cultural developments in both German states following the war. The general character of the two societies was utterly dissimilar, to be sure: on the one hand, a proletarian order where the working classes set the tone, were given ideological pride of place, and received unprecedented opportunities for education and professional advancement; on the other, a consumer-oriented "leisure" society dominated by the middle classes. Whereas the old economic and educated middle-class elites lost their power and position in the GDR, those in the Federal Republic were largely able to weather the halfhearted denazification efforts of the late 1940s.

But there were undeniable similarities as well, as the comportment and grievances of East and West German youths suggest – and not just when it came to rearmament. On both sides of the Iron Curtain lived "hooligans" (*Halbstarke*) who sported ducktails and adored jazz and rock, as well as other disillusioned, dispassionate youths – the "skeptical generation" identified that decade by West German sociologists.[11] But that was where the similarities ended. There would be no equivalent in the GDR to the youth rebellion that rocked the Federal Republic in the late 1960s, even if state security officials seemed to believe that their own "beatniks" and "rowdy" youths posed a serious domestic threat to the regime. In the end, that generation's failure to erupt in the East as it did in the West spoke volumes about the differences between the two states: about the possibilities for expressing discontent publicly and thus about the infinitely more repressive nature of the GDR – notwithstanding accusations in the West about Adenauer's "authoritarian" tendencies.

There were other important societal parallels as well, not least in the agricultural sector. The relative economic importance of farming and the percentage of the population that toiled the land declined significantly in both states. Massive flight to urban centers, especially by young people, reflected a desire for more "modern" amenities and lifestyles, as well as for higher earnings in the industrial sector. This was a global phenomenon after 1945, yet East German officials characteristically blamed "hostile" forces intent on undermining the economy. It is doubtful that "class enemies" were unwitting agents of modernity in the GDR. Still, there was a major difference when it came to the driving force behind these similar sectoral and demographic shifts. Only in the GDR did political and economic discontent about forced agricultural collectivization – the poor performance of the new collective farms, the loss of independence they entailed – drive young people from the land.

The position of women revealed other similarities lurking just beneath ostensible social differences. East German authorities proclaimed early on the principles of equal rights and equal pay for both sexes, and they strongly encouraged women to enter the labor force. Ideology played an important role here, but even more significant were economic considerations tied to the challenges of reconstruction and the need to make up for severe manpower shortages, especially as more and more East Germans fled to the West.

Working women nevertheless faced a good deal of everyday discrimination in the GDR in terms of pay and possibilities for promotion; many also experienced sexist hazing by male colleagues.

The situation was much different for women living in the Federal Republic, but not because of more progressive policies or mores. Rather, traditional gender roles quickly re-emerged in the West, where most women were forced out of the workforce and back into the role of homemaker at the end of the war, to make room for returning soldiers and the "denazified." Those who remained in the labor force were criticized by conservatives and the churches in both states, especially if they were working mothers. In different ways, then, East and West German women continued to experience the same types of patriarchal treatment common before 1945 – an important sign of historical continuity and yet another parallel between the two postwar societies.

There was no societal "zero hour" on the shop floor either, where traditional hierarchies had more or less survived the war.[12] Official propaganda in the East about new forms of socialist ownership was, in many respects, just that: propaganda. The regime certainly courted and claimed to rule in the name of manual workers, who advanced to positions of power in many factories and enjoyed other forms of preferential treatment – even if, in the end, politically correct behavior counted more than one's social pedigree for getting ahead.

Still, East German workers were handled with kid gloves by functionaries concerned about maintaining domestic peace and satisfying the almighty Plan, especially following the mass uprising of June 1953. That was why production quotas remained artificially low, and why, in turn, increases in wages regularly outpaced those in productivity. Workers in the West, for their part, enjoyed a greater say in the running of their factories, thanks to the introduction of "codetermination" (*Mitbestimmung*), a new practice that allowed them to delegate representatives to the highest levels of management.

But it was still clear in both states who gave and who followed orders, who made and who carried out important policy decisions. "What was the main difference between communism and capitalism?" went a joke that made the rounds in the GDR, where the same issues that had perennially soured industrial relations in Germany and elsewhere – earning levels, long hours, and poor working conditions – remained volatile sources of discontent, even though the "means of production" now supposedly belonged to the people: "Capitalism is the exploitation of man by man. And communism is the exact opposite!"[13]

The Search for Stability

The "long 1950s" began with the official founding of the two German states in 1949 and climaxed with the erection of the Berlin Wall in August 1961.[14] This was a decade of conspicuous contrasts: a time of dismantling and reconstruction, both economic and political, cultural and moral; a time of "Americanization" and "Sovietization"; a time of upheaval amid a desperate search for stability. These were the years that cemented the division of the former Reich, both literally and figuratively, as the two halves of Germany drifted away from each other and became integrated – politically, economically, militarily, socially, and culturally – into two hostile camps, the capitalist West and communist East. Yet, there was never a complete separation, even as the concept and meaning of the nation-state were reappraised.

Despite serious concerns at the time, it turned out that Bonn was *not* Weimar, and a number of factors made this so: the Federal Republic's strong economic performance, which helped sustain its generous welfare state policies while reducing social and class antagonism; its successful economic, cultural, political, and military integration into the community of Western nations – in contrast to Germany's destabilizing pariah status after World War I; the gradual emergence of a stable political system dominated by a handful of moderate and mainstream parties working under the provisions of a new and improved constitution. All of this was abetted by the very existence of the Federal Republic's fraternal rival in the East, which helped rally many West Germans to their state by forging an anticommunist consensus grounded in fear, especially following the Berlin Blockade and the crushed uprising of June 1953.

In short, the Federal Republic may have been "dull" and unspectacular, but it quickly enjoyed the popular legitimacy that had proved so elusive during Weimar. Konrad Adenauer had given most West Germans what they most wanted: peace and prosperity. And that was why he could run so successfully on the campaign slogan "No Experiments" in the federal elections of 1957, which resulted in the first and only absolute majority for a single party in the history of the republic.

There were different reasons for the stability of the GDR, whose lackluster economy often failed to satisfy even the most basic needs of the populace, whose leadership could not make entirely good on its generous social welfare promises, and whose citizens, for the most part, remained cool – if not outright hostile – toward Sovietization, their country's exploitative economic integration into the Eastern bloc, and a government that lacked democratic legitimacy. The regime nevertheless managed to survive the severe crises of the 1950s, including the upheaval of 1953 and the human hemorrhage that eventually led to the construction of the Berlin Wall.

What, despite widespread dissatisfaction, held East Germany together – or at least prevented it from falling apart? Repression, fear, and obedience certainly played a role, even if they failed to stop East Germans from taking to the streets en masse in June 1953. But that was not all. Apathy and withdrawal, the successful flight of the more disgruntled to the West, the efforts by many low-level officials to appease those under their charge by responding to their demands and grievances: all of this also played a significant role by weakening the potential for opposition. In the end, of course, East German officials resorted to more vigorous measures to keep their state intact. The Berlin Wall punctuated the final division of postwar Germany as well as the end of the "long 1950s." This may have shored up the stability of the GDR, but the price for that, at least for the time being, was the German nation itself.

3
Consolidation (1961–1972)

The construction of the Berlin Wall began shortly after midnight on August 13, 1961 – a day that would live in infamy for Germans on both sides of the Cold War divide. The ruling SED scurried to justify the brutal measure, euphemistically dubbing it an "antifascist protective barrier" solely intended to keep out "class enemies" intent on destroying the GDR. Whatever the preferred terminology, the concrete monstrosity tore apart families and friends, neighbors and communities: an entire city, in short – to some, the German nation.

Over the next decades, hundreds would die trying to escape to the West. It was a sad but revealing commentary on the socialist project's failure to achieve legitimacy in the eyes of most East Germans, who now found themselves corralled and completely cut off, physically, from the West. Scholars and pundits have described the drastic decision as a "second" or "secret" *refounding* of the East German regime.[1] One thing is certain. It gave the unpopular SED state a fresh lease on life by stopping the human hemorrhage that had threatened to sap the GDR of all its vitality.

At the same time, the Wall "solved" the German Question for the foreseeable future. A series of international summits dedicated to this perennial source of stress took place in the second half of the 1950s, and a number of prominent public figures – including Polish foreign minister Adam Rapacki and American diplomat George Kennan, the father of "containment" – put forth provocative proposals calling for some sort of united but neutral Germany. None came to fruition. By the 1960s, the dominant international players had relegated the German Question to the proverbial backburner in the wake of the Wall, the escalating conflict in Vietnam, and, last but not least, the Cuban Missile Crisis. That dispute in the Caribbean, which brought the world to the brink of nuclear war and gave Moscow a foothold in the Western hemisphere, produced a precarious stability – a stalemate of sorts, another *cementing* of the status quo, so to speak – following the forced enclosure of West Berlin. Each of the Cold War blocs now had its own "island" deep within the other side's territory.[2]

Adenauer's Fall and the *Spiegel* Affair

Just as the East–West showdown in Cuba was reaching its height in October 1962, a crisis erupted in the Federal Republic that put a final nail in Konrad Adenauer's political coffin: the so-called *Spiegel* Affair, which punctuated a political decline that had already set in. Advanced in age, obsessed with maintaining power, and perhaps drunk on the political success he had enjoyed since 1949, the wily politician committed a series of serious missteps following the CDU's astounding victory in 1957. These included a bizarre announcement to run for the office of federal president, a clumsy attempt to create a second public television station more supportive of government policies, and an abysmal public-relations fiasco: his failure to visit West Berlin in a show of solidarity following the construction of the Wall.

Even Adenauer's foreign policy achievements at this time – like his efforts to improve relations with France by befriending and working closely together with its strong-willed president, Charles de Gaulle – were overshadowed by domestic disagreements. So-called Atlanticists, who placed greater value on a strong relationship between West Germany and the United States, did their best to undermine a major accord the two leaders signed in the early 1960s: the Elysée Treaty, which marked a highpoint of rapprochement between the two "hereditary enemies," France and Germany.

Calls for Adenauer's resignation reached a crescendo in the fall of 1962 following his government's ham-fisted response to a critical report in *Der Spiegel* about alleged shortcomings in the country's military capabilities. The arch-conservative minister of defense, Franz Josef Strauss, had the offices of the influential weekly newsmagazine searched, ordered the arrest of its editors, and subsequently lied to the Bundestag about his involvement in this scandalous episode. That proved too much for the FDP, the CDU/CSU's junior partner in the governing coalition. Its leaders wrung a concession out of Adenauer, who agreed to step down as chancellor exactly one year later, in October 1963.[3]

Critics who had long complained about the chancellor's authoritarian style not only felt vindicated but also saw the government's strong-arm tactics as a dangerous sign of backsliding. Perhaps, but the large-scale public protests that erupted in defense of press freedom attested to just how far many Germans had left the Nazi past behind them – a prelude to the wave of social and political liberalization that would take place in West Germany later that decade.

The GDR in the 1960s: Reforms in the Shadow of the Wall

A different type of wave washed over East Germany at the time. Secure in the shadow of the Wall, communist authorities unleashed a torrent of repressive measures, including a huge spike in politically motivated arrests and even the introduction of forced labor camps. This was the time to push through regime policy, no matter how unpopular. After all, what recourse did the disgruntled now have?

That repressive wave soon gave way to an era of economic reform and cultural thaw, though this, too, did not last very long. In January 1963, East German leader Walter Ulbricht announced a raft of far-ranging reforms aimed at raising productivity and efficiency. Brimming with buzzwords that would become increasingly familiar to East Germans, the so-called New Economic System (NES) promised to correct the "mistakes" of the past by introducing a variety of measures aimed at "modernizing" the economy and "rationalizing" the production process.

To that end, it called once again for a "scientific-technological revolution" based on the introduction of cutting-edge technology and automation. It also emphasized the need to train a new, technically proficient elite capable of applying more "scientific" management methods, like cybernetics. An equally important component of the economic reform program gave state-owned factories more say over production decisions and greater interest in making a profit because they could now use it for reinvestment. Economic planning was to be more decentralized, in short, and fulfillment of the almighty economic plan less important.

This was accompanied by the introduction of a more permissive climate in the cultural realm. Artists and writers were given greater freedom to be more independent and openly critical, to address divisive, burning social issues – a taste of Mikhail Gorbachev's *glasnost* avant la lettre. There were other palpable changes besides the chance for more open debate: a series of amnesties for political prisoners, the removal of statues celebrating Stalin, and greater opportunities for previously non-privileged groups under state socialism, like the children of *non*-manual laborers, to study at university.

The reforms paid off, at least initially. There was a noticeable increase in productivity and an improvement in the standard of living, as income levels rose and more consumer durables became available. East German film and fiction also flourished, as new talents like directors Frank Beyer and Konrad Wolf, authors Christa Wolf and Stefan Heym, became household names. Yet, all of this proved short-lived. By the end of 1965, the SED had partially reversed its economic reforms and revoked its liberal cultural policies. East German artists and intellectuals had apparently gone too far in their criticism – just as their Chinese counterparts had done a few years earlier during Mao's Hundred Flowers Campaign.

Greater economic decentralization seemed an equally dangerous challenge to the party's political control. That, along with financial problems and the consequent neglect once again of consumer goods, made it painfully obvious that the reforms had not lived up to official expectations. The GDR was one of the world's most industrialized countries, to be sure. But in terms of productivity levels and general prosperity, it continued to lag far behind the Federal Republic, making even more laughable Walter Ulbricht's audacious if illogical promise in 1969 that the GDR – whose ramshackle, poor-quality cars were the butt of many jokes – would blow past and "overtake" the West German economy without even pausing first to "catch up."[4] The West German labor force continued to enjoy a shorter workweek, higher real income, larger retirement pensions – as well as faster, better-quality, and technologically more advanced automobiles. By 1970, almost a quarter of all West Germans owned cars; the figure was well below 10 percent in the GDR, where individual East Germans had to wait many years before their coveted Trabant or Wartburg finally rolled off the assembly line.[5]

The New Economic System turned out to be a dismal disappointment, in short. To make matters worse, the winter months of 1969–70 were among the coldest and snowiest on record in almost a century. Shortages of food and energy reached alarming levels, even by GDR standards, as a result of the severe weather conditions and accompanying production backlogs. This gave rise once again to a great deal of popular discontent. In an ironic allusion to the celebratory festivities that had just marked a milestone in the history of the postwar socialist state, disgruntled East Germans mocked at the time: "No coal in the basement, no potatoes in the sack. Long live the twentieth anniversary" of the GDR.[6] This was the final nail in the coffin of Ulbricht's reform program – *and* of the communist leader's own political career, it turned out.

Widespread anger about a material situation reminiscent of the immediate postwar years was entirely understandable, especially in the wake of the recent if modest improvements associated with the economic reforms of the mid-1960s. The preceding period may have been a "golden age," relatively speaking, but a short-lived one. Was this a "missed opportunity" to save the GDR, as some scholars claim? Perhaps, but one that likely had as little chance of success on that score as the Stalin Notes of 1952.[7]

Student Revolt and Reform from Above

The GDR may have surpassed its neighbors in the Soviet bloc in economic and material terms, but that offered little solace to ordinary East Germans, who seldom looked eastward when assessing their own living situation. The yardstick, also for their leaders, remained the Federal Republic, which still enjoyed a comfortable economic lead. But not all was rosy there, either.

In the mid-1960s, after more than a decade of high growth rates and low unemployment figures, the "economic miracle" experienced its first hiccups. A recession began in 1966, and a year later, the GDP fell slightly for the first time since the war. Inflation accompanied an uptick in unemployment, all resulting from a variety of structural challenges, such as declining birth rates and the cutting off of labor from the GDR following the construction of the Wall. The latter showed just how entwined their histories were and continued to be.

Ludwig Erhard, the architect of the *Wirtschaftswunder* and Adenauer's successor since the fall of 1963, proposed a series of tax hikes to deal with an increasingly dire budget situation. That proved too much for the economically liberal FDP, which withdrew from the governing coalition in protest. A so-called Grand Coalition consisting of the largest parties – the CDU/CSU and the SPD – took over the reins of government in December 1966, led by conservative politician Kurt Georg Kiesinger, a past member of the Nazi Party. Former mayor of West Berlin and lifelong Social Democrat Willy Brandt, who had spent the Third Reich in exile in Norway, served as the new foreign minister.

How did a coalition government formed by the country's main political rivals come about? The path to the seemingly impossible had begun almost a decade earlier. In 1959, two years after its trouncing at the polls in federal elections, the SPD adopted a new program at a gathering in Bad Godesberg, a quaint spa town in the Rhineland right beside the West German capital. The party's focus on socialist economic policies such as nationalizations, and its opposition to Adenauer's policies of Western integration at the cost of national unity, did not sit well with most West German voters, who were privy to the dismal example of state socialism and menacing Soviet occupation right next door.

The new program represented a major break in the strategy and approach of the near-century-old workers' party, which had once been the largest and strongest in all of Europe. By banishing Marxism from its political agenda and distancing itself from its more unpopular policies, the SPD hoped to reach beyond its traditional base and become a "catch-all" people's party – just as the CDU had attempted to become a "catch-all" party for German Catholics *and* Protestants following centuries of religious and cultural antagonism.

In an ironic twist, the country's largest progressive protest movement took shape not long after a leftist political party had come to power for the first time since 1945. Ironic perhaps, but not altogether surprising. The two developments were intimately linked. The trigger was proposed legislation known as the Emergency Acts, which the Western Allies had demanded in return for granting full sovereignty to the Federal Republic. The controversial law would have set limits on a variety of freedoms, including the right to strike and demonstrate. Other basic rights, including the privacy of personal communications like mail and telephone calls, also seemed to be under attack, redolent of contemporaneous practices in the GDR. But the proposed strictures also brought to mind Article 48, the infamous section of the Weimar constitution that gave the president emergency powers and was used in the early 1930s to undermine the first functioning democracy on German soil. Others compared it to the Nazis' Enabling Act of March 1933, which spelled the definitive end of the democratic constitutional order and the rule of law. Whichever historical analogy was most apt, the past *and* present continued to weigh heavily.

There was, as noted, a straightforward connection between the rise of the protest movement and the SPD's ascension to power. A Grand Coalition meant that there was no effective voice in the Bundestag to oppose the laws, so protest formed *outside* parliament: an "extra-parliamentary opposition" composed mainly of disaffected students, writers, other leftist intellectuals, and the unions. Large-scale opposition to unpopular government policies was nothing new. There had been major protests against remilitarization and plans to equip the Bundeswehr with nuclear weapons in the 1950s, and then against the government's high-handed actions during the *Spiegel* Affair in the early 1960s. But the SPD had played a leading role in those protests. Because it was now a member of the government, the initiative fell to others.

The clash about the Emergency Acts coincided with – and gave a boost to – developments in West German society that were less ostensibly political in nature. Like elsewhere in the West, this period witnessed the emergence of new attitudes, values, and lifestyles, especially on the part of youths increasingly critical of the aspirations and practices of the postwar "affluent society."[8]

There was a certain irony here. For one, the security that came from that very prosperity had made it possible for baby boomers to adopt such critical attitudes in the first place. Besides, West German youths were certainly not averse to material acquisitions, as their consumption of fashionable clothes and rock-and-roll music attested. But the seemingly crass materialism and strait-laced sexual mores of their elders became increasingly suspect in a "postmaterial" age of "free love." There were many reasons for this, but one factor fueling this growing "generation gap" was a widening "education gap," as university study became more accessible to traditionally excluded socioeconomic groups in the 1960s – the reverse, ironically, of what had taken place in the GDR following the construction of the Wall (see p. 80).

A more immediate trigger for the protest movement was a growing sense of frustration on the part of the so-called sixty-eight generation of college students about overburdened universities, manned by conservative professors and unbending administrators woefully unprepared for the sudden influx of a more diverse group of students – and about the ongoing conflict in Vietnam. The brutal war in Southeast Asia, and the Federal Republic's support for America's role there, galvanized a generation and seemed to confirm inchoate suspicions that something was seriously rotten about the state of West German democracy.

Such misgivings found expression in – and were partly inspired by – the theoretical musings of social scientists associated with the so-called Frankfurt School, who drew on Marx and Freud to launch a potent criticism of modern capitalism and conformist bourgeois society. "Structural" continuities with the Nazi period, they argued, along with the perilous allure of "mass" (read: American) media, culture, and consumption, contained the seeds of incipient fascism. The Federal Republic was, to put it crudely, an accident waiting to happen. Again.[9]

There were ironies here, too, especially when it came to views about the political and cultural influence of the United States. After all, the country condemned for Vietnam and the spread of "trash" culture was the very same country whose youths had first taken to college campuses to fight for civil rights and against "imperialism," serving as a model and inspiration for West Germany's "sixty-eighters." It was also the same country, incidentally, whose political and military leaders had tried in vain, twenty years earlier, to institute many of the educational reforms now demanded by West German students.

Anti-Americanism was no invention of the postwar period, to be sure. But criticizing one's erstwhile liberator and "morally superior" protector must have provided some solace to young Germans who felt guilt and shame because of the Nazi period. The same might be said, incidentally, of staunch leftist criticism of Israel following the brief but fateful war of June 1967. This is not to gainsay necessarily the validity of their criticisms. Besides, the sixty-eight generation reserved its greatest moral condemnation for those closer to home: older Germans who had failed to act during the 1930s and 1940s.

The West German students were part of a worldwide campaign against authoritarianism, imperialism, and other anti-democratic tendencies. But one aspect of their protest differentiated it from the ones taking place elsewhere: its distinctive focus on their country's dark past. How had the Third Reich been possible, members of the sixty-eight generation wanted to know. What had the older generation done to stop or, worse, abet Hitler and his henchmen? And why, many youths angrily asked, had their elders and teachers swept the past under the proverbial rug after the war?

This narrative – that progressive youths suddenly discovered the horrors of the 1930s and 1940s in the late 1960s – is familiar but misleading. Nazis' crimes, especially against the Jews and other persecuted groups, were certainly not a major preoccupation during the first two postwar decades. Past *German* suffering was. But already beginning in the late 1950s and early 1960s, one detected signs of a less defensive, more open and critical reckoning with the recent past, largely through legal, cultural, educational, and scholarly channels.

There were a number of reasons for this, beginning with a disturbing spate of antisemitic activity at the time. Officials created a central office charged with investigating Nazi-era crimes and bringing to justice those who had gotten off earlier with no more than a slap on the wrist. The first exhibitions and memorial sites were set up at former concentration camps. German artists, writers, and intellectuals published a number of searching studies, biting theatrical pieces, and critical essays.

There were external pressures and influences as well. The East German regime launched a propaganda campaign to expose former Nazis still in prominent positions of power in the West, and Israel brought Nazi bigwig Adolf Eichmann to justice in a widely watched trial in Jerusalem. The so-called Frankfurt Auschwitz trials took place soon thereafter, marking the first time *Jewish* suffering was a major theme in the West German media.

All of this laid the groundwork for "sixty-eight." But there was one major difference. Defiant youths now readily invoked the Nazi period to criticize what they found repressive and objectionable in the Federal Republic, not least at schools and universities. Drawing on the teachings of the Frankfurt School, they detected contemporary parallels to Nazi atrocities everywhere. This gave rise to the use of inflated rhetoric and analogies intended to impugn political elites and call attention to purported "fascist" continuities between the Third Reich and West Germany. It may also explain why the provocative but nonviolent tactics initially adopted by the "extra-parliamentary opposition" eventually gave way to more violent ones: a semiconscious attempt, perhaps, to make up for the failure of their elders to use force to resist Hitler?

There was a more immediate trigger for the turn to strong-arm tactics: a series of violent run-ins between West German officials and young demonstrators, beginning in June 1967, when a policeman shot and killed a student in West Berlin at a demonstration protesting a state visit by the autocratic Shah of Iran. Thus began a decade of violence that included an attempt on the life of Rudi Dutschke, one of the more charismatic and articulate student leaders – just one week after a sniper had gunned down Martin Luther King, Jr., in early April 1968. The ensuing paroxysm of violence peaked that spring, especially against the Springer Press, a conservative news empire that had been mercilessly goading the protesters. In late May, the Bundestag adopted a toned-down version of the Emergency Acts. The controversial legislation was passed, but the heavens did not darken.

That seemed to take the wind out of the would-be revolutionaries' sails. Equally important was the adoption of a series of conciliatory policies by a new coalition government formed in the fall of 1969 by Willy Brandt's Social Democrats and the liberal FDP. This marked the first time the Christian conservatives were excluded from power. In response to many of the criticisms and demands voiced during the protest movement, Brandt declared that his government would push through a series of political and social reforms that would break with received authoritarian traditions and "dare more democracy."[10]

More concretely, he announced an array of domestic reforms, including greater equality between the sexes in family and marriage law, pension reform, and an increase in welfare benefits and social entitlements. The new Social–Liberal coalition identified greater democratization, liberalization, and modernization as its goals – even as countercurrents appeared on the horizon: new state regulatory policies, for example, and the adoption of a so-called Anti-Radical Decree intended to remove members of the extreme left from public positions of power via vetting processes that measured one's commitment to the constitution. Taking with one hand what it gave with the other, such policies seemed at variance with Brandt's calls for greater democracy and individual freedom.

Détente and *Ostpolitik*

Whatever the shortcomings or inconsistencies of his domestic reforms, Brandt is best remembered for his foreign policy – above all, his efforts to reduce tensions with the Soviet bloc. The new chancellor's *Neue Ostpolitik* (New Eastern Policy), the West German contribution to détente, was the primary focus of his first years in office. It came in recognition that the hardline approach, pursued by his predecessors to undermine the GDR and bring about unification, had failed. The various strands of that policy had been subsumed under the so-called Hallstein Doctrine, first formulated by high-level diplomats in the mid-1950s. In line with West German claims to be the sole representative of the German people, the Federal Republic refused to recognize the GDR or maintain diplomatic relations with the Soviet satellite. But that was not all. In an effort to isolate its rival internationally, Bonn refused to establish – and even threatened to cut off

– diplomatic relations with any state that did so, an effective pressure tactic given the country's economic might. The West Germans refused, more generally, to recognize the postwar status quo: not just German division, but also the new borders established in Eastern Europe after 1945, that is to say, the loss of the country's prewar territories in that region.

The Wall made it brutally clear that this "policy of strength" had failed and that nothing was going to change any time soon, and the Cuban Missile Crisis reminded Germans and the world about the very real danger of a nuclear conflagration. Soviet tanks deployed to Czechoslovakia in the late summer of 1968 to suppress the Prague Spring also made it obvious there would be no change in the East in the foreseeable future. All of this initiated a process of reassessment – also of the perennial German Question. But it was not by chance that Brandt was the driving force behind Ostpolitik. As mayor of West Berlin when the Wall was built, he was intimately familiar with the very real *human* costs of division – for those living in the GDR and for West Germans with friends and relatives beyond the concrete divider.

Faced with a fait accompli, the goal now was to do anything possible to improve the situation and minimize the suffering of East Germans who had not made it to the West. And that meant a greater willingness to compromise and reach some sort of arrangement with communist authorities. "Change through rapprochement" (*Wandel durch Annäherung*) became the new catchphrase, a term coined by Brandt's close confidante and adviser Egon Bahr as an alternative to the hardline Hallstein Doctrine.[11] The new approach dangled concessions – piecemeal recognition of the GDR and the existing borders in Eastern Europe – in return for everyday humanitarian improvements and greater freedoms for those living under the yoke of state socialism.

Like the sixty-eighters' calls to face the Nazi past, Brandt's diplomatic démarche also had a prehistory. Journalists began earlier that decade to make a case for recognition in the national media, economic feelers with the Soviet bloc led to the creation of trade missions in the East, and official agreements made it easier for certain individuals to make short-term visits between East and West. A string of East German diplomatic successes in the so-called developing world meant, just as important, that the writing was on the wall. The Hallstein Doctrine was no longer an effective form of economic blackmail to impede international recognition by other countries. In fact, for the first time, the GDR was permitted to send its own team to the Olympics in 1968, where it won more medals than its West German rival did. Though tainted by notorious doping practices, the country's undeniable athletic prowess eventually became a source of pride to many ordinary East Germans – as well as a means for their state to gain greater international legitimacy.

There was another factor at play. Because of Soviet tensions with China and their increasingly volatile rivalry for leadership of the communist world, Moscow was now prepared to make concessions to the West. East German leaders feared, for their part, that Ostpolitik was a thinly disguised Trojan horse and that any truck with the Federal Republic would ultimately come at the GDR's cost – just as many in Bonn had long feared the superpowers reaching some sort of disadvantageous deal over the heads of both German states. In a sense, this was the (West) Germans taking things into their own hands. And their Western allies, especially in Washington, were anything but enthusiastic.

Brandt's government signed two treaties in 1970 – one with Moscow, the other with Warsaw – that renounced the use of force and declared the postwar borders in the East "inviolable" – stipulations reminiscent of the Locarno Treaties of the 1920s. The Poles were especially keen to have the West Germans recognize the Oder and Neisse Rivers as Poland's western borders. This set the stage for an agreement between the two postwar German states. Following a series of high-level, high-profile meetings – including a visit by Willy Brandt to the GDR, where he was enthusiastically greeted by crowds of ordinary East Germans – the two states signed the so-called Basic Treaty in 1972, just days before Christmas.

Sharply breaking with policies stretching back more than two decades, each side formally recognized the other, with self-determination and unification remaining an option at some point down the road

– a concession demanded by the West Germans. Additional agreements were reached over Berlin, with an eye to reducing tensions further in the divided city, the symbolic focal point of the Cold War. The Wall remained standing, but travel between the two halves became easier, especially for Westerners wishing to visit friends and family in the East. Brandt acknowledged that there were "two states in Germany" but insisted they were not "foreign countries" to one another.[12] This "special relationship" found expression at the diplomatic level. Instead of formal ambassadors and embassies, they exchanged "permanent representatives" housed in "permanent missions."

West German conservatives were incensed. They considered any recognition of an "illegitimate" state that had committed grave crimes against its own citizens – against fellow Germans – to be a sellout. The arch-conservative Springer Press would only refer to the GDR in quotation marks, suggesting that it was neither German, nor democratic, nor a republic. Equally angry were those who had fled or been expelled from their homes in the former eastern territories. But as Brandt memorably pointed out, nothing there had been lost that had not been "gambled away" by Hitler and the Nazis long ago.[13]

Much like Mikhail Gorbachev two decades later, Brandt became a beloved international figure, often compared to John F. Kennedy at the time because of his youth and photogenic good looks. His spontaneous genuflection at the Warsaw Ghetto Memorial, during a visit to Poland in 1970, won praise from abroad. This unplanned gesture was especially meaningful because Brandt himself bore no personal guilt for past German crimes. A staunch opponent of the Nazis, he had gone into exile during the Third Reich, something that gave him greater credibility in the "antifascist" East. That solemn expression of atonement was more controversial back home, just like Ostpolitik as a whole.

Whatever the mixed domestic response, the Brandt government would go on to survive the first constructive vote of no confidence in West German history (see p. 34). A half year later, in November 1972, the SPD–FDP coalition won early federal elections, seen by many at the time as a referendum on Ostpolitik. Walter Ulbricht's fate was less rosy. His openness to Brandt's overtures, coupled with the recent failure of his economic reforms, alienated Moscow and other East German leaders. The Soviets unceremoniously removed him from office a year and a half later, following a power struggle in the Politburo led by his political protégé Erich Honecker, who became the new East German leader in the spring of 1971.

What was the upshot of Ostpolitik? The Federal Republic gave up its stubborn claim to be the sole representative of the German people; the GDR, for its part, was finally able to cast off its pariah status and win international recognition. Both states joined the UN in 1973. Contact normalized between their leaders and even became somewhat easier between ordinary citizens who found themselves on different sides of the Cold War divide. The possibility of unification remained on the table, but at some indeterminate point in the future.

In a sense, Ostpolitik was a preliminary peace treaty ending World War II two decades before an actual one was finally signed following the fall of the Berlin Wall. The status quo – German and European division – had been confirmed, tensions over border issues largely defused. The German Question was resolved, at least for the time being, and attention turned to extra-European conflicts in the "developing world." Fears that Germans would once again try to dominate Europe and the world had dissipated, if not entirely disappeared. Allies and protectors in both Cold War blocs continued to pay lip service to some vague promise of German unity one day down the road, but, if pressed, most shared the sentiment of French novelist François Mauriac, who had once quipped, "I love Germany so much I'm glad there are two of them."[14]

More German–German Parallels and the German Question

In different ways, the focus of Brandt's foreign policy and that of his predecessors had been the German Question. Their stated goal was essentially the same – unification – but their approaches could not have been more dissimilar. For Adenauer, freedom for West

Germans and their integration in the "free world" – one day as citizens of a fully sovereign state on equal footing with its allies – came before unity *but* was seen as the best path to achieve that long-term goal. Successful Western integration allowed Brandt to set a different accent and offer another solution, especially in the wake of the Wall: How to increase freedom and improve the daily lives of East Germans *and* one day bring about unification? A rigid "policy of strength" gave way to a more flexible attempt at "change through rapprochement." Which of the two ultimately led to the end of national division – and the Cold War as a whole – is a question that historians will long debate.

Other concerns besides the German Question came to dominate West German discourse in the 1960s: how to fortify liberal democracy at home and create a more socially equitable society while preventing another world war that might lead this time to German incineration. These issues were especially important to members of the younger, "Westernized" generation, who considered the "national question," "the nation," and unification less pressing. They were not a focus of the sixty-eighters, a "postmaterial" and, in a sense, "postnational" generation. The case was different for older Germans, who had been socialized differently and thus remained attached, not least emotionally, to the idea of a German nation. Those in the GDR who looked westward for salvation, or who had strong personal or familial ties on the other side of the Elbe, also felt differently – even as Walter Ulbricht floated the idea of a separate "socialist nation" in the East, a concept later anchored in the GDR's third constitution of 1974.[15]

Historic, cultural, and linguistic ties aside, it was nevertheless clear by the 1960s that the two societies were growing apart, that the bonds connecting them were growing weaker. Some identify the events surrounding "sixty-eight," which had no equivalent in the GDR, as the point where the two societies really began to diverge, with the Federal Republic becoming more liberal and democratic – and eventually unfathomably richer. The West German economy recovered from the doldrums of the mid-1960s by the time it became clear at the close of the decade that Ulbricht's economic reforms had failed so miserably. A "post-material" lifestyle may have been an option for young people living in the prosperous West. East Germans, for their part, were still waiting on long lines to acquire even the most basic goods.

All of this coincided, ironically, with the emergence in the West in the 1960s of a popular set of ideas known as "convergence theory," which claimed that modern industrial societies like East and West Germany were becoming more and more alike. Political and ideological differences would recede in importance, the argument went, because these societies were adopting similar strategies – such as "rational," scientific, technocratic solutions – in response to the complex but common challenges of "late modernity."[16] West German authorities even (tentatively) embraced state planning in the 1960s – ironically, just as their East German counterparts began experimenting with less centralized forms of economic decision-making.

Following the Sputnik shock of 1957, technological achievements suggested to some in the West that Soviet-style regimes were doing something right, something worthy of emulation and recognition, not unlike the USSR's transformation under Stalin – at great human cost, of course – into a leading industrial power. West Germans did not wish to abandon the free market per se, but they did hope to "improve" it – just like certain members of the East German intelligentsia who had called for reform in the wake of Khrushchev's destalinization campaign in the mid-1950s: to improve state socialism, not do away with it.

There were other parallels between the two states in the late 1960s, especially in the social realm – ones that often get lost in the welter of obvious political and economic differences. Homosexuals would continue to experience various forms of discrimination in East and West Germany, to be sure, but both states did remove from the books at this time a century-old provision of German criminal law ("Paragraph 175") that strictly forbade sex between men. Divorce laws evolved along similar lines as well, with less emphasis on "guilt" as a reason for marital dissolution. Both states also adopted more liberal abortion laws at the time, leading to a spike in the termination rates of marriages *and* embryos. More women joined the labor force in the GDR, which suffered from chronic shortages of workers and staff, and many were becoming more independent than their counterparts in the West. But working women on both sides of the Elbe continued to experience rabid sexism, not least at the workplace. Conservatives and church representatives on both sides of the Elbe balked at working mothers, who, they insisted, should remain at home to clean, cook meals, and raise children.

Those children, especially ones from the lower socioeconomic classes, now had increasing access to higher education, also in both states. The need to accommodate them led to a West German boom in the construction of new high schools (*Gymnasien*) and universities, formerly bastions of the middle and upper classes. There was also a noticeable uptick in East German housing construction that decade, mainly to make up finally for wartime damage and the dilapidated state of prewar stock after years of neglect.

There was no "sixty-eight" in the GDR, but there were comparable social tensions and forms of resentment. Generational conflict was more visible in the Federal Republic, but older Germans in the West *and* East complained about supposedly lazy, insolent, and unkempt youths, whose common affinity for American-style music and clothing was considered anathema. Conservative West Germans feared some sort of "communist plot," whereas true believers in the East suspected a concerted effort to subvert the socialist project. America's malevolent cultural influence was nevertheless one thing they could all agree on.

No "genuine" convergence that decade, then, despite some important social and economic parallels. That process would first begin two decades later, in 1989–90. But the path to eventual political and economic unification started with the diplomatic developments of the Brandt era. Contacts between those living on either side of the Wall increased, to be sure, but for the time being, West German society as a whole turned even further away from the East and focused more on the West – and on itself. For all the homegrown criticism of the Federal Republic during the tumult of the late 1960s, there was a new but palpable sense of pride in the many accomplishments of the West German "model."

Political scientist and journalist Dolf Sternberger referred to this as "constitutional patriotism" (*Verfassungspatriotismus*), a term later popularized by philosopher and sociologist Jürgen Habermas.[17] But this newly felt attachment went beyond just acceptance of and admiration for – a greater sense of identity with – the liberal, democratic constitution and institutions of the Federal Republic. Its economic success, its generous social welfare policies, its growing social and cultural openness, also its greater willingness to confront the crimes of the past: all of this gradually won over West Germany's most vociferous domestic critics – though not all, as an alarming wave of domestic terrorism in the 1970s would soon make clear enough. Still, given the role that a lack of loyalty had played in the destabilization of Weimar and the rise of Hitler and the Nazis, this was an encouraging development indeed.

4

Crisis (1973–1989)

There was good reason for optimism in both German states at the start of the 1970s. Living standards had markedly improved since the end of World War II. The economy and infrastructure had largely been rebuilt following wartime ravaging. Though still behind its West German rival, the GDR had the strongest economy in the Soviet bloc, and the Federal Republic had recovered from a worrisome recession in the mid-1960s. Its economy was booming again, with annual growth rates above 5 percent and unemployment below 1 percent.

Things were looking up for both countries on the world stage as well. Thanks to Willy Brandt's Ostpolitik, the GDR was on the path to gaining international recognition beyond the Iron Curtain, and its citizens could look forward to greater contact with friends and relatives in – and consumer items from – the West. As for Brandt, the chancellor's diplomatic overtures won him the Nobel Peace Prize in December 1971. West German writer and pacifist Heinrich Böll even received the organization's prestigious prize in literature the following October, the first time a German citizen had won the award since 1929. In the early 1970s, Germans clearly had a great deal to celebrate. Had they finally put their past behind them?

Böll's achievement was overshadowed by a horrific event that had taken place one month earlier in September 1972, when members of a militant Palestinian organization murdered a dozen people in Munich: eleven members of the Israeli Olympic team and a West German policeman. It was not just the tragic loss of life that shocked West Germans. They had hoped the Munich Olympics would showcase their country's accomplishments as a "modern," prosperous, and peaceful democracy – precisely thirty-six years after Hitler had presided over the Berlin Games in 1936.[1] Instead of demonstrating just how much their country had progressed since the war, the twenty-hour hostage standoff was, in hindsight, an omen of what was to come over the next decade and a half: terrorism and domestic strife, economic and environmental crisis, much of which was tied wholly or in part to shifting developments in the Middle East.

The "Two Helmuts" and the End of the "Thirty Glorious Years"

For decades, the Federal Republic had relied for much of its energy needs – almost 60 percent by the early 1970s – on inexpensive oil from that troubled region, much as the GDR and the rest of the Soviet bloc had long received cheap, subsidized oil from the USSR.

But in the wake of the Arab–Israeli war of October 1973, prices shot up when the oil-producing states of the region decided to weaponize their valuable natural resource by cutting back on deliveries to Western nations that had come out in support of Israel.

That would have important knock-on effects for the West German economy, exacerbating another hit it had recently taken. Two years earlier, in response to increasing foreign trade deficits at home, US president Richard Nixon had announced the end of the Bretton Woods Agreement that had regulated the international currency market and fixed exchange rates since the end of World War II. This was significant because it led to an increase in the value of the previously undervalued deutschmark, making West German exports more expensive – and thus less desirable – on foreign markets. There was another major reason for the drop in exports, namely, increased foreign competition, especially from Asia, in economic sectors where the Germans had long excelled, such as steel and other heavy industry.

Other structural factors contributed to West Germany's economic woes, but the upshot of the oil embargo was a full-blown economic crisis that affected all the industrial nations of the West. Its main features were slower and even negative economic growth rates, inflation, and rising unemployment. Growing indebtedness also became a matter of concern, as officials increased public spending to cushion the blows to the economy and workforce. The West's "thirty glorious years" of postwar recovery had seemingly come to an end.[2]

This was, indeed, more than just a "cyclical downturn." A combination of stagnating economic growth and inflation was something the modern world had never seen, and economists even coined a new word to describe it: *stagflation*. Just as the old terms could not capture the character of this new challenge, the traditional economic remedies did not work either. This compelled governments to devise new ones. In West Germany, that task fell to Social Democrat Helmut Schmidt, who became chancellor when Willy Brandt was unexpectedly forced to resign in the spring of 1974 after it was discovered that an East German spy had infiltrated his inner governing circle.

Brandt's fall from power and grace was a political shock. Known and respected worldwide for his opposition to *both* German dictatorships, the Third Reich and the GDR, his reformist policies had helped promote peace and stability at home and abroad, contributing in no small measure to postwar Germany's political and moral rehabilitation – not least in the eyes of many youths. His successor was made of different stuff. A former officer in the Wehrmacht and an economist by training, Helmut Schmidt represented the more conservative, "no-nonsense" wing of the SPD, boldly embracing the free market and adopting a more authoritarian, sometimes supercilious style that alienated younger, more progressive members of his party.

Like elsewhere in the West, Schmidt's ascension to power marked the end of Keynesianism, the dominant economic approach of the postwar period. In its stead came a variety of policies intended to combat inflation and reduce state debt by tightening the money supply and reining in spending on social welfare benefits. Monetarism and austerity were the new buzzwords, supplemented by additional ones under Schmidt's successor, Helmut Kohl: deregulation and privatization.

A consummate politician and trained historian, Kohl became head of the CDU in 1972. Under his leadership and following its trouncing at the polls that year, the conservative party embraced policies intended to broaden its appeal to voters beyond its core constituency. That strategy eventually paid off, and in 1976, the CDU enjoyed its strongest electoral performance in almost two decades – but Kohl would still have to wait another six years before becoming chancellor.

In the fall of 1982, Schmidt's government lost a constructive vote of no confidence in the Bundestag when the economically liberal FDP decided to leave the coalition after calling in vain for greater cuts in social spending. That decision led to the exodus of its more leftist-leaning members, but it allowed the party to play the role of "kingmaker" once again, joining a new government that October led by Helmut Kohl. In the neoliberal mold of Ronald Reagan and Margaret Thatcher, his coalition pushed for lower taxes on businesses, greater investment incentives, and more "personal responsibility" in response to the continuing economic malaise, made worse by a second oil crisis in 1979. But there was a major difference. In contrast to the Americans and British, Kohl did not try to dismantle the social welfare state or declare war on the unions. To that extent, there was a great deal of continuity following the political shake-up of the early 1980s. That was also true, as we shall see, when it came to relations with the East.

The upshot, under Schmidt and Kohl, was that the West German state came to play a somewhat reduced role in running the economy, whose workings were increasingly left to the invisible hand of the market – within limits. For one, attempts to control spending by freezing or lowering welfare benefits were offset by a variety of state expenditures intended to cushion the blow of structural challenges that had led to the decline of certain sectors: retraining the now unemployed, propping up and subsidizing the hardest hit segments of the economy (such as the coal industry), and investing in new industries. These policies paid off by the mid-1980s, resulting in lower levels of inflation, a more balanced budget, as well as higher exports and a hugely favorable trade surplus.

Unemployment nevertheless remained high, suggesting there was only so much any single government could do, given the nature of the crisis and the increasing interconnectedness of the world economy. That was why Germany and the other member states of the EEC looked to closer ties in Europe as a remedy for the economic downturn ushered in by the "oil shocks" of the 1970s. Greater European integration received an initial shot in the arm under Helmut Schmidt, who reached important agreements with French president Valéry Giscard d'Estaing aimed at harmonizing their countries' economic and currency policies. But it was especially under Helmut Kohl, starting in the mid-1980s, that the move toward a more united Europe – including baby steps on the path to a common currency – really gained momentum.

Fears outside the Federal Republic about the strength and influence of the deutschmark, as well as West German economic domination more generally, propelled this process. But economic considerations were not the only driving factor. Concerns about the perennial German Question resurfaced in the wake of Ostpolitik – more specifically, concerns that the Federal Republic might become neutral or, more disconcerting, return to the century-old habit of wavering between the East and West to advance *German* interests. In theory, greater European integration would offset the specter of a new *Schaukelpolitik* ("seesaw policy") by tying Bonn even more tightly to its postwar partners in the West.

At the same time, closer economic ties and the addition of new EEC members – Denmark, Ireland, and the UK in 1973; Greece, Portugal, and Spain the following decade – boded well for West German exports. Domestic developments in France – above all the departure of President Charles de Gaulle from the political stage in 1969 – played an important role here by removing major impediments to greater cooperation and enlargement. In fact, France and the Federal Republic would increasingly become known as the "motor" of European integration. Starting in the 1970s, political consultations among European heads of state became more frequent, and the number of joint European projects flourished. These included the founding of the multinational aerospace corporation Airbus in 1970 and the European Space Agency in 1975. Such ventures helped offset the prohibitively high costs of new technology, allowing European manufactures to become more competitive on the world market.

Helmut Kohl was a more vigorous proponent of European integration than his immediate predecessor, and his pro-European outlook helped the EEC overcome several seemingly intractable impediments, including the fraught issue of European cash subsidies for hard-hit farmers – especially French ones. This involved enormous outlays, largely subsidized by West German taxpayers, given the Federal Republic's preponderant economic position in Western Europe. This was not unusual. To move past various financial impasses, Bonn frequently assumed a disproportionate share of the financial burden – just as it would take in a disproportionate number of refugees in the following decades.

This was not driven solely by feelings of altruism or guilt about the Nazi past. Europe's strongest economy stood to gain from accelerated economic integration. In fact, Bonn desired closer political integration as well, but this met with resistance, especially in Paris and London. Still, Kohl successfully championed the Single European Act of 1986, the first major revision of the Treaty of Rome since the birth of the European Community almost thirty years earlier. It paved the way to the creation of a true single market the following decade by removing almost all trade barriers among the member states. It was also an important step toward one day achieving closer political cooperation, foreign-policy coordination, and, eventually, a single European currency.

Atomic Anxieties

In a more direct and immediate response to the "oil shock" and other economic challenges of the 1970s and 1980s, the Federal Republic began to focus more intently on the search for alternative forms of energy. Germany's first nuclear power plant had already gone online and began producing electricity in the late 1960s, long before oil prices or shortages were an issue. By the time a second oil shock began in the wake of the Iranian revolution of 1979, there were almost two dozen commercial reactors in operation, funded by the state and supplying roughly 5 percent of all domestic energy needs. That was certainly more promising, in the long run, than the government's initial response to the OPEC embargo of 1973: a short-lived ban on Sunday driving and the temporary introduction of speed limits on the famed autobahn.

Such measures had proved unpopular – certainly on the part of disgruntled car owners fond of driving as fast as their automobiles would allow on roads initially constructed four decades earlier under Hitler. But the turn to nuclear energy as a solution to the oil crunch also raised the ire of a growing segment of West German society concerned about industrial pollution and the damage it was inflicting on the environment.

The environmental movement that took shape in the 1970s had antecedents. Earlier in the century, German conservatives and more leftist "friends of nature" had expressed similar concerns about the relentless pursuit of "progress" and other supposed ills associated with the dawn of "modernity." But in the 1970s and 1980s, it was especially (but not solely) "progressives" on the Left who embraced such values. Alarmed by the visible damage to heavy industrial regions and the phenomenon of forest dieback (*Waldsterben*), a new generation of environmentally conscious individuals demanded a dramatic reduction in the consumption of raw materials – and in consumption more generally. Physical and mental health, "self-realization," and other "quality-of-life" matters mattered more to them than limitless economic growth and prosperity.

Just as the economic remedies of the past were ill equipped to combat the scourge of stagflation, there was a sense that the new environmental challenges of the present required novel responses and forms of protest. Disenchanted with the established political parties, heeding Willy Brandt's challenge to "dare more democracy," and following in the footsteps of the extra-parliamentary opposition of the 1960s, activists began to form "citizen initiatives" that embodied a new kind of "grassroots democracy" (*Basisdemokratie*). Embracing direct action from below, they focused on the recent turn to nuclear energy as a substitute for coal and oil, largely because of fears about the dangers of radioactive contamination, meltdowns, and the disposal of spent fuel rods.

The release of Hollywood movies like *China Syndrome* and accidents like the one at Three Mile Island in Pennsylvania – less than two weeks apart in March 1979 – did more than just fuel and confirm such fears. They provided retroactive justification for earlier, often violent protests that decade against the opening of new atomic plants in Germany. The creation of storage facilities for radioactive waste, like the controversial one in Gorleben in Lower Saxony, was another serious bone of contention.

Opposition to atomic energy coincided with the end of détente and coalesced with the "Euromissile debate" of the late 1970s. Détente had reached its climax with the signing of the Helsinki Accords by members of both Cold War blocs in the summer of 1975. The so-called Final Act represented a major international compromise, with the West recognizing the political and territorial status quo in Europe in return for a public commitment on the part of the Soviet-bloc states – including the GDR – to respect human rights at home. But within just a few years, this high point of détente gave way to a new phase of the Cold War.

It was none other than Helmut Schmidt who got the ball rolling. In the fall of 1977, the West German chancellor publicly denounced the USSR's recent deployment of a new class of short-range SS-20 nuclear missiles in Eastern Europe, claiming that this had undermined the strategic balance in Europe. Two years later, in December 1979, NATO officials responded to this challenge by adopting the so-called Double-Track Decision, which threatened to deploy a new class of American nuclear missiles in Western Europe ("track two") if a fresh round of arms negotiations ("track one") were to fail. The prospect of a new arms race touched a raw nerve, especially in the Federal Republic (and the GDR), where apocalyptic fears of a third world war – this time a nuclear confrontation, *on German soil*, no less – were especially intense.

This was reminiscent of the late 1950s, when a broad coalition of concerned West Germans had protested the stationing of atomic weapons on German soil. The outrage seemed even greater this time, if measured solely by numbers. Hundreds of thousands took to the streets, and in a throwback to the so-called Göttingen Manifesto of 1957 (see p. 67), some 5 million Germans would eventually sign the 1980 Krefeld Appeal, a statement demanding that the government withdraw its support for the deployment of new Pershing II missiles in Western Europe. Opposition extended to leading members of the chancellor's own party, who even demanded that the Federal Republic withdraw from NATO – yet another throwback to the 1950s. Ronald Reagan's fiery Cold War rhetoric, first as a candidate, then as president, only heightened the hysteria.

The popular West Berlin band Nena released the international antiwar hit, "99 Red Balloons," in March 1983, and the protest reached a crescendo that October, when more than a million demonstrators joined peace marches across West Germany – the largest wave of demonstrations in the history of the Federal Republic. The Bundestag voted in favor of the Double-Track a month later, and the first Pershing II was stationed soon thereafter in the Federal Republic.

Terrorism and the Rise of the Greens

It was at this point that the protest movement began to fizzle out, much as earlier ones had when faced with a fait accompli. But that did not mean it left no traces. For one, it led to the rise of the Green Party, which would become a major political force in Germany over the next years – despite (or because of) its members' evident disdain for parliamentary politics "as usual." Disarmament and pacifism, feminism and the environment: these were the new party's core issues, and several of its founding members quickly became media darlings at home and abroad – none more so than Petra Kelly, its first leader in the Bundestag.

Just three years after its founding, the Green Party entered the parliament in 1983, its representatives carrying twigs and potted plants. The party had convincingly cleared the constitutional 5-percent hurdle by securing almost 6 percent of the vote. By the end of the decade, the upstart party would have representatives in all state legislatures, thanks to support from urban areas and college towns, as well as from progressive baby boomers, academics, and other members of the anti-authoritarian "alternative milieu." The "anti-party's" nontraditional style – rotating leadership rules, gender quotas, and informal attire in the Bundestag (jeans and sweaters in lieu of jackets, skirts, and pantsuits) – clearly appealed to its growing constituency of typically better-off and more educated supporters.

Members of the established parties might have looked askance at their new colleagues. Today's Greens probably would have as well! But whatever hackles they and their "antics" initially raised, the party played an invaluable role in helping to bring attention to environmental issues. Just as important, it helped defuse social *and* political tensions in the Federal Republic by giving voice to an increasingly alienated segment of the electorate. The Greens also provided a home for many in the alternative milieu who had earlier turned to terror to vent their anger and bring about fundamental change.

The first acts of political violence took place in the late 1960s, at the height of the student protest movement. The use of force became closely associated with the Red Army Faction (RAF, aka Baader–Meinhof Gang), a militant group of "romantic" communist revolutionaries that officially formed in 1970. Embracing armed struggle and inspired by the guerrilla tactics of Third World liberation movements, various iterations of the RAF carried out bombings, kidnappings, and even assassinations against prominent representatives and symbols of the West German political, economic, and conservative media establishment.

The climax came during the so-called German Autumn of 1977, which began in late July with the murder of Jürgen Ponto, the head of the Dresden Bank. That September, members of the "second generation" would kidnap and later execute Hanns Martin Schleyer, the president of the German Employers' Association (and a former SS officer during the Third Reich). They hijacked a Lufthansa plane a month later, in a desperate attempt to free imprisoned members of the "first generation." A crack counter-terrorist team created in the wake of the Munich Olympics fiasco stormed the *Landshut* in Mogadishu, Somalia, shot the hijackers – who had ties to the Palestine Liberation Organization – and freed the remaining hostages after a five-day ordeal that had kept West Germans glued to their radios and television sets.

Whatever sympathy some moderate leftists in the Federal Republic may have felt for the goals (if not extreme methods) of the RAF, support quickly dissipated after the fall of 1977 – as did extreme-left radicalism as a whole. Maintaining stability in the face of such militant challenges was no mean feat, but the Federal Republic managed to survive the political and economic trials of the 1970s and 1980s – from stagflation and high unemployment to terrorism and urban youth riots, from environmental degradation to a series of corruption scandals at the highest levels of government and politics. Democracy and the rule of law remained intact and, in contrast to the Weimar period, won over most West Germans, not just politically but also emotionally. European integration, the social market economy, as well as "Western" cultural norms and tastes were all widely embraced.

By the 1980s, the Federal Republic had become a more pluralistic, liberal, and cosmopolitan society: a "normal" place, in short, similar in most respects to its West European neighbors – also, alas, when it came to the scourge of racism and xenophobia, *despite* renewed efforts to deal more openly with the Nazi past.

"Coming to Terms" with the Past

The violent events of the mid-1970s eventually gave way to more peaceful methods of protest. But they did have at least one lasting effect: a significant increase in state surveillance, strong-arm police methods, and the collection of personal data to avert similar attacks in the future. This triggered criticism that the "fascist" West German state was finally showing its true face – the goal, of course, of the would-be revolutionaries and their chosen methods. There were also overblown claims that repression was the same on either side of the Wall. That collapsing of distinctions was ironic, as we shall see, because it was *precisely* at this juncture that the intensity of state surveillance increased exponentially in East Germany, largely in response to Ostpolitik and (prescient) fears about the potentially harmful effects of greater contact with the Federal Republic.

Claims about incipient "fascism" had been common during the student protest movement of the late 1960s. But it was in the late 1970s and especially the 1980s that interest in Germany's dark past really gathered momentum. Temporal distance and generational shifts played a role here. So, too, did a series of spectacular media events that brought the Nazi past front and center: the airing of the popular American miniseries *Holocaust* in early 1979, for example, and the publication a few years later of fraudulent "diaries" supposedly written by Hitler. It was at this point that interest in the genocide of the European Jews finally became the focus of intense – often intensely emotional – public debate in the Federal Republic.

That produced a series of backlashes, also at the highest levels of government. Upon assuming the chancellorship, Helmut Kohl and his advisers hoped to instill a greater sense of national self-confidence and self-respect by reminding their fellow Germans, especially members of the younger generation, that there was more to their nation's past than just its twelve darkest years. Germany was, after all, not just a land of soldiers and spies but also "poets and thinkers," and their achievements in the arts, culture, and sciences were world-class. But a number of ill-chosen official comments and other public missteps undermined the new chancellor's efforts to create a more positive sense of historical identity. These included a highly controversial visit on May 5, 1985, with President Ronald Reagan to a military cemetery in the city of Bitburg, where former members of the Waffen-SS were also buried. This prompted accusations by the Left that the chancellor and other conservatives were trying to whitewash the past.

Three days later, German president Richard von Weizsäcker, former mayor of Berlin and a liberal member of Kohl's party, commemorated the fortieth anniversary of his country's defeat in World War II by delivering a remarkable – and much remarked upon – speech that helped reverse some of the damage. In it, he acknowledged in no uncertain terms Germany's historic responsibility for Nazi crimes. Weizsäcker commemorated "in particular" the persecution and murder of European Jewry, as well as that of other groups systematically oppressed by the Nazis. What's more, he characterized the military loss not as a defeat but as a "day of liberation," a highly controversial claim at the time (and a curious choice of words, given that the term was usually associated with the freeing of survivors from the Nazi death camps). The speech was a watershed moment, in any event, and it helped set the stage for the infamous "historians' controversy" (*Historikerstreit*) of the mid-1980s: a fierce public debate that began a year later between prominent progressive and conservative intellectuals and academics about the causes and supposed singularity of the Holocaust.[3] It was at this point that the genocide of the Jews became sacrosanct, regarded by most West Germans as the measure of all evil, *the* essence of Germany's recent past.

"Guest Workers" and Political Xenophobia

Claims that conservatives were attempting to "repress" or "relativize" the past coincided with another alarming development at the time: the rise of political xenophobia. In the late 1960s, West German industry redoubled its efforts to recruit "guest workers" (*Gastarbeiter*) from abroad: largely unskilled laborers who were only supposed to remain for a short time in the Federal Republic – as "guests," so to speak. This came in response to the economic rebound of the late 1960s. But there was another reason: West German industry faced labor shortages following the construction of the Wall, which had ended the flow of refugees from the GDR. Recruitment campaigns had first begun during the "economic miracle" of the late 1950s, with workers coming mainly from the less well-off European "periphery": Italy, Greece, Yugoslavia, and, increasingly, Turkey. The oil shock of 1973 and the ensuing economic crisis brought this to an abrupt halt.

Recruitment may have ended, but most of these workers remained in the Federal Republic, frequently joined from abroad now by their families. Stubbornly insisting that Germany was not a "land of immigration," authorities did little to help integrate those planning to stay for the long haul. Instead, they offered them incentives to return to their native countries – largely in vain. As a result, these impoverished, poorly educated, low-skilled migrants remained apart – socially, culturally, and often linguistically – and their very foreignness made them a source of suspicion and resentment.

Foreign workers had already experienced xenophobia in the 1960s, but it became even more widespread and intense over the next two decades, especially in an era of stagflation and high unemployment. Fearful of competition for jobs and resentful of the social benefits enjoyed by these workers, those Germans who were suffering most became increasingly susceptible to the appeal of right-wing, xenophobic parties making gains across much of Western Europe at the time.

A massive increase in the number of global refugees added fuel to the fire by producing a huge spike in applications for political asylum in the late 1970s. West Germany was a popular destination because of its material prosperity, generous social welfare policies, and the fact that it had one of the world's most liberal approaches to asylum. Intended as a form of "atonement" for Nazi crimes, Article 16a of the West German constitution guaranteed asylum to any "persons persecuted for political reasons."[4] But with the rise of Political Islam, global terrorism, and a surge in the number of refugees from nonindustrial, non-European states, the radical (and later mainstream) right made convenient scapegoats of the new asylum-seekers, stylizing them as "bogus" "economic refugees" coming for purely venal reasons. This led in the 1980s to the first violent attacks against refugee living quarters – a trend that would only get worse following unification in 1990.[5]

"Real-Existing Socialism" and the Stasi under the "Two Erichs"

Foreign laborers experienced similar social exclusion in the GDR, where thousands of so-called contract workers (*Vertragsarbeiter*), mainly from Vietnam and Mozambique, arrived in the 1980s. There were other parallels. For one, these migrants *also* came in response to labor shortages, a perennial bugbear of the East German economy. Almost 100,000 were living in the GDR the year the Wall fell, housed in separate lodgings and generally kept isolated from ordinary

East Germans. Family members were not permitted to join them, in contrast to the situation in the Federal Republic, but in both states, these workers usually ended up filling highly undesirable, labor-intensive jobs that most ethnic Germans were loath to perform.

Keeping foreign workers separate from the native population was not the only form of "isolation" practiced in the GDR. Concerns about the potentially destabilizing effects of détente resulted in a series of official policies intended to keep out "malevolent," Trojan horse-like Western influences. These efforts at greater "demarcation" (*Abgrenzung*) from the West took various forms starting in the early 1970s, but it was in the realm of state surveillance that the weightiest and most fateful changes took place. Erich Mielke, who had headed the Stasi since 1957, joined the Politburo, the regime's true locus of power, as a full member in the spring of 1976 – a first for any leader of the Ministry for State Security.

That was not the only indication of the organization's new stature. To ward off the West's pernicious influence in the wake of Ostpolitik, its size and reach increased dramatically starting in the early 1970s. Between 1971 and 1989, the number of full-time Stasi officials doubled, and the net of "unofficial" informants and collaborators – ordinary East Germans who spied on friends and family, neighbors and colleagues – widened significantly as well. Out of a population of roughly 16.5 million, roughly a quarter million East Germans worked for the Stasi in some capacity the year the GDR imploded. Tens of thousands of political prisoners were incarcerated, and hundreds died trying to flee to the West. The Federal Republic may have been "full of Nazis," as the East Germans long claimed, but in the end, it was the repressive GDR regime whose practices more closely resembled those of the Third Reich.

Besides the growth in sheer numbers, the methods of the Stasi evolved considerably over the GDR's final two decades. Instead of cracking down on "undesirable" behavior *after* the fact, it adopted increasingly sophisticated methods aimed at nipping challenges to the regime in the bud. That was why it was so important to widen the web of informants, whose numbers gave rise to the popular but misleading impression that the Stasi was omniscient and omnipresent. However exaggerated, that perception effectively helped defuse the potential for unrest. In fact, many East Germans would later use this to justify their low levels of civil courage before 1989 – even if the greatest and only successful grassroots challenge to the regime since the state-wide uprising of June 1953 would take place *precisely* when the Stasi was at the height of its power in the late 1980s.

Like most autocracies, the East German regime did not just rely on "sticks." It also used "carrots" to keep the populace in check – just as it had in the wake of the Wall. Soon after grabbing power from Walter Ulbricht in 1971, with Moscow's blessing, a different Erich – Erich Honecker – announced a series of important reforms intended to win the hearts and minds of ordinary East Germans – or at least keep them docile. East Germans were to enjoy the fruits of socialism in the here and now, not, as long promised, at some indeterminate point in the future. Consumer goods and housing received greater priority, as a result, with *social* policy gradually eclipsing *socialist* policy.[6] There was a marked liberalization in the cultural realm as well. Censorship was eased, as part of this "cultural thaw," and there were to be no prohibitions or "taboos" in the arts and literature.

East German youths, whom security officials considered one of the greatest threats to domestic stability, benefitted immediately. The regime was now more tolerant, within limits, of Western influences that young East Germans found so appealing, such as long hair and rock music, *Nickelbrille* (John Lennon-style, metal-rimmed glasses), and *Nietenhose* (jeans). As Edgar Wibeau, the protagonist of Ulrich Plenzdorf's wildly successful 1972 novel, *The New Sorrows of Young W.*, put it, "Jeans are an attitude, not just trousers."[7] A year after the Munich Olympics, East German leaders similarly tried to present a different, less "grey," more upbeat image of the GDR. At the World Festival of Youth and Students, held in East Berlin in the summer of 1973, hundreds of thousands of East German youths had the opportunity to listen to pop music and mingle with visitors from almost 150 countries, including leftist westerners like the American political activist Angela Davis.

"Red Woodstock" would long remain a bright memory for many young East Germans. But what they and their elders would recall even more fondly from this period was the attention suddenly given to improved living standards and everyday consumption levels. Still traumatized by the events of June 1953 – and in the wake of a severe supply crisis in the GDR, as well as recent protests in neighboring Poland set off by price hikes – East German officials announced in the spring of 1971 that better material conditions would be the "main task" of the latest five-year economic plan. This new focus on the here and now, on "consumer socialism," went beyond mere promises to make desired consumer goods more available. Higher wages, increased social benefits (especially for newly married couples and large families), as well as intensified building construction were now all on the agenda.

This was the era of the *Plattenbau*, prefabricated, cement-slab housing projects intended to solve once and for all the endemic shortage of adequate lodging. West Germans might have looked with disdain upon the concrete jungles that began to dot the GDR's landscape at the time, even though they could have just as easily found similar "housing estates" built in the new "international style" on the peripheries of their own urban centers. The drab uniformity of the East German *Plattenbau* nevertheless came to symbolize for many in the West an inhumane system with no regard for human individuality.

Yet, for those East Germans forced to live in older, dilapidated buildings with few or no modern comforts, these were highly desirable dwellings well worth waiting for. And wait they did – but not just for new apartments. By the 1980s, roughly a third of all East German households owned an automobile. By contrast, the corresponding figure in the Federal Republic was 65 percent. But East German cars like the iconic Trabant ("Trabi") or more luxurious Wartburg were vastly inferior to their West German counterparts. To add insult to injury, frustrated buyers usually had to wait a dozen or more years before their cars finally rolled off the assembly line – unless they had "connections."[8]

Basic goods like housing, heating, and food were heavily subsidized and therefore relatively inexpensive, often leading to unnecessary waste. But because shortages continued to be commonplace, long lines in front of stores staffed by sullen salespeople remained a familiar sight, especially when word spread that a desired commodity had suddenly become available. This was why it was so important to have "contacts," especially relatives and friends in the West – the easiest way to obtain scarce, exorbitantly priced "luxury" goods only available for hard (that is, Western) currency in so-called specialty stores that had first opened in the 1960s and 1970s following the construction of the Wall. Access to dollars and especially deutschmarks was the key to consumer satisfaction, but also an important marker of socioeconomic inequality. This led to much resentment and grumbling, especially in a state whose leaders had promised to eliminate unfair socioeconomic differences.

The standard of living for most East Germans did indeed improve noticeably following the fall of Ulbricht. But the same old deficiencies caused by economic planning and state socialism – apathy and poor morale at the workplace, chronic absenteeism and low productivity, labor shortages and excessive overtime – meant that everyday reality continued to fall far short of the elevated expectations engendered by official promises. To make matters worse, a 1971 decision to nationalize all remaining private enterprises, including those run by independent craftsmen, created serious supply chain disruptions that contributed further to chronic scarcity.

Even so, living standards in the rest of the Soviet bloc paled in comparison to those in the GDR. But its citizens did not compare their lot to that of their counterparts in Eastern Europe. Their benchmark was life in the Federal Republic. A source of envy, to be sure, but West German wealth and prosperity did have certain immediate advantages for those stuck on the other side of the Wall: massive Western loans, for instance, which the regime used to purchase coveted goods from abroad and finance the regime's generous social policies. But there was a clear and dangerous downside to all this, to living beyond one's means: trade imbalances and mounting foreign debt – a major reason why the regime would eventually collapse.

The mounting economic crisis was just *one* final nail in the coffin of "real existing socialism," a term that entered official parlance in the 1970s. Increasingly bold criticism of the regime was another. Pursuing policies introduced a decade earlier in the wake of the Wall, Honecker encouraged writers, artists, and intellectuals to voice constructive criticism about inauspicious developments in the GDR. This eventually produced another backlash, just as it had in December 1965, when none other than Honecker himself had gone on the attack against those who had gone "too far."[9]

This time, East German leaders decided to send a clear message by targeting singer-songwriter Wolf Biermann, whose popular, catchy, and bitingly satirical songs about life in the GDR had long been a thorn in the side of the regime. While he was out of the country on tour in the West in November 1976, the regime announced that it had revoked his citizenship. This produced a great outcry, culminating in a public declaration of protest by dozens of prominent East German intellectuals and artists – a first in the history of the GDR.

The cultural thaw ended abruptly, once again, but not this time the ferment from below. A year later, in 1977, a highly critical text appeared in the West, written and smuggled out by an East German dissident, Rudolf Bahro. *The Alternative* made the case for a more homespun, grassroots path to socialism different from the one propagated by GDR officials.[10] In the fall of 1979, a year after being sentenced to prison, Bahro was unceremoniously deported to the West. This was now the regime's preferred way to deal with unwelcome critics: force or allow them to leave for the West, usually in exchange for hefty payments by the Federal Republic – in coveted Western currency, of course.

Getting rid of the disgruntled in this way was more than just an important source of hard currency, or valuta. It also served as a safety valve – but it did not eliminate all discontent. In fact, a grassroots peace and environmental movement emerged in the early 1980s, inspired, in part, by similar developments in the West. Its ranks included members of the "countercultural" milieu that had coalesced in large urban areas like Berlin, Dresden, and Jena, as well as committed leftists who hoped to salvage socialism by "reforming" it – just like party loyalists who had called for systemic reforms in the wake of Nikita Khrushchev's destalinization campaign a quarter century earlier *and* like Mikhail Gorbachev just a few years later. Often finding refuge in local Protestant churches headed by sympathetic pastors, they engaged in activities that served as a training ground for the protest movement that would sweep away the regime later that decade.

Encouraged by the Helsinki Accords and similar to their counterparts in the West, East German critics focused on disarmament, adopting as their slogan the biblical pacifist catchphrase "swords into ploughshares." They, too, viewed nuclear war and environmental degradation as the most imminent threats to humankind. It was not by chance that the so-called Berlin Appeal of 1982 – a grassroots, East German declaration calling for neutrality, demilitarization, the withdrawal of occupation troops, and a ban on nuclear weapons on the territory of *both* German states – closely echoed the demands of the West German Krefeld Appeal of 1980.[11] The Chernobyl nuclear accident of 1986 only confirmed such fears on both sides of the Iron Curtain.

Youths and Women in the Two German States

Fear and ferment from below were not the only parallels between the two postwar Germanies in the 1970s and 1980s. Vulnerability to the vagaries of foreign fuel prices was another, as were efforts on both sides of the Wall to make up for labor shortages by recruiting foreign workers. The latter, as we have seen, experienced similar social isolation in *both* states. Concerns about improving the image of each country abroad were a further commonality, as were attempts from on high to forge a closer connection between state and society by fostering a more positive civic identity: a purely "socialist" one in the East, a more "patriotic" one in the West.

Here, youths remained of special concern to authorities. Though less obvious in the GDR, an "alternative" youth milieu took shape on both sides of the Wall after 1968, one that embraced remarkably similar values and lifestyle choices that frequently served as a substitute for more traditional forms of political activism: a belief in individualism and self-fulfillment, coupled with a strong dose of anti-authoritarianism and a desire to live beyond the confines of mainstream (bourgeois or socialist) society. Western-style skepticism, pessimism, and a "count-me-out" (*ohne-mich*) attitude found their counterpart in East German apathy and a widespread desire to escape official pressures to conform by fleeing into private "niches" – developments that could be traced back to the 1950s in both societies.

There were important parallels, too, when it came to the position of women, as we saw in the previous chapter. Since unification in 1990, the idea that those in East Germany had been somehow more "emancipated" than their counterparts in the West has enjoyed wide currency. What is beyond dispute is that women had come a long way since the 1950s – in *both* states. The percentage of women in the GDR labor force or enrolled at university was impressive by the 1980s, among the highest in the world. But the advances made by West German women, including married ones, were nothing to sneeze at either. By 1990, for example, the percentage of men and women pursuing higher degrees was roughly the same in the Federal Republic.

Gender roles had evolved considerably since 1945, to be sure, leading to a noticeable shift in traditional family structures, including an uptick in the number of single mothers. Both states introduced policies aimed at lightening the load of working mothers, assuming responsibilities and tasks traditionally borne by the family. Daycare and maternity leave may have been more generous and more widely available in the GDR, but West Germans also benefitted from such policies.

This continued to elicit pushback in both societies – yet another important parallel: by the socially and politically conservative in the West, by those (men) in the East who remained impervious to the regime's official commitment to gender equality. As a result, pay levels and the percentage of women in leading positions lagged considerably behind those of men. The distribution of household chores tended to follow traditional patterns, too, resulting in a "double burden" for East and West German women who worked both inside and outside the home. Greater independence clearly had its limits.

The parallels between the two societies are, in hindsight, as striking as the differences – no surprise, given mutual cross-border influences, as well as the fact that both states faced similar challenges in an increasingly interconnected, postindustrial world. Still, the two Germanies would soon experience very different fates.

The Road to Collapse

At the start of the 1980s, almost no one foresaw the fall of the Berlin Wall, the collapse of the GDR, or the end of the Cold War – all within a decade! There were, to be sure, hints about what was to come: the Solidarity movement in Poland, for example. But few things were further from anyone's mind when the decade began. The Cold War had entered another ice age, with the Soviet invasion of Afghanistan and a "new" missile crisis, followed by a series of proxy wars in Africa and Latin America. Détente ended abruptly, just a few short years after Helsinki, and international affairs became more complicated in other ways as well. With the rise of Political Islam, a new multipolar world emerged, with fault lines running not just between East and West but also North and South, as Moscow's ill-fated adventure in the Hindu Kush made clear.

That conflict could not have come at a more inopportune time for the USSR. Under Khrushchev's successor, Leonid Brezhnev, the Soviet Union had settled into an extended period of social and economic stagnation. This set the stage for the political rise of Mikhail Gorbachev, a robust reformer who assumed the reins of power in the late winter of 1985. In response to the many structural challenges the USSR faced, Gorbachev introduced a raft of new policies intended to salvage Soviet-style communism. They led instead to its collapse, in his own country *and* in Eastern Europe. *Glasnost* (greater political transparency), *perestroika* (economic and administrative restructuring), and disarmament were the three main prongs of his reform program, with the last – a reduction in arms spending – intended to pay for the others.

All of this had direct economic and political repercussions for the GDR and the other members of the Soviet bloc. For decades, the USSR had supplied its client states with cheap, heavily subsidized oil – for the Eastern European economies, one of the few benefits of belonging to the Council for Mutual Economic Assistance (Comecon). Prices now rose, for a variety of reasons, and supply levels were severely reduced over the course of the 1980s, only adding to the region's existing economic woes. For the GDR, this was a final straw.

Always precarious, its economy became increasingly insolvent, largely a result of poor policy choices. Besides a failed foray into the production of microchips and other microelectronics, East German leaders stubbornly stuck to traditional industrial sectors at a time of global decline, not least in terms of demand. That, along with decreasing productivity, technological inferiority, low-quality manufacturing, and decrepit infrastructure, resulted in an increasingly lopsided trade imbalance by the end of the decade.

To make matters worse, the GDR was living beyond its means. Pressure to increase social benefits and satisfy consumer demand at home grew dramatically with greater exposure to Western prosperity, thanks to Ostpolitik. This resulted in a huge increase in consumer imports from the West, made possible only through enormous Western loans and credits – including ones from the Federal Republic to the tune of billions of deutschmarks. Kohl and other West German conservatives had put aside their earlier opposition to Ostpolitik, especially after the electoral drubbing of 1972, and embraced its pragmatic efforts to improve the quality of life for ordinary East Germans.

The SED walked a fine line, accepting heaps of economic aid from the West at the same time it strove to ward off "subversive" cultural and political influences. Such assistance was important because it gave the GDR a desperately needed lifeline – not to mention a clear advantage over the other Soviet-bloc states (much as a stipulation in the 1957 Treaty of Rome had exempted trade between the Federal Republic and the GDR from customs duties, essentially giving the East Germans backdoor access to the European Common Market).

Many in the West even believed – falsely, it turned out – that the East German economy was stronger than that of the UK, that its industry was the eleventh largest globally. In fact, it was on the verge of collapse. But fearful of losing control and averse to antagonizing the populace, the country's leaders were not willing to introduce the sort of reforms that might have provided crucial economic relief. As chief SED ideologue Kurt Hager craftily put it in an interview about Gorbachev's policies, which appeared in the spring of 1987 in a West German newsweekly, "If your neighbor changes the wallpaper in his flat, would you feel obliged to do the same?"[12]

That was an astounding rebuff, and an ironic one.

Just as the East German "masses" had finally found something of value in the old SED slogan, "To learn from the Soviet Union means to learn victory," their own leaders had suddenly become more skeptical. Just as astonishing was Gorbachev's announcement at the time that each socialist country could choose its own path. That was an implicit renunciation of the so-called Brezhnev Doctrine, which had held, since the suppression of the Prague Spring, that a threat to socialism in one socialist state was a threat to socialism in all states – and thus demanded a (military) response. Few recognized it at the time, but the GDR's days were numbered.

The German Question was not on many minds, then, as the decade drew to a close. Few Germans – or foreign observers, for that matter – expected to see unification in their lifetime. But after reaching a nadir in the early 1980s, relations between the two German states did improve. Trade increased and visits by high-level officials and even ordinary Germans were on the rise. Thousands of political prisoners were allowed to leave for the West – ransomed in exchange for hard currency.

What's more, West German authorities, hoping to forestall the type of political instability recently seen in Poland with the rise of Solidarity and the imposition of martial law in 1981, provided the GDR regime with massive loans in exchange for token improvements in human rights. Indeed, critics would later accuse Bonn and the mainstream parties of propping up the regime economically – and politically, too, by refusing to have much truck with East German dissidents, while welcoming Honecker to the Federal Republic with full state honors in the fall of 1987.

In exchange for that last concession, Kohl's ceremonial remarks were broadcast live on GDR television. Unity remained a "goal," the chancellor declared, but quickly added that the "German Question" was "not currently on the agenda of world history." In the winter of 1989, Hans-Ulrich Wehler, a leading West German historian, went a step further, jauntily explaining to a large audience at Yale University the reasons "Why Germany Must Remain Divided."[13] Nine months later, the Berlin Wall came toppling down and the German Question was once again on the international agenda.

5

Dis-Unity (1989–1998)

If one had to choose a single date that captures the vicissitudes of twentieth-century German history, it would be November 9. Kaiser Wilhelm II was forced to abdicate on that day in 1918, just hours before a republic was proclaimed in Berlin. Five years later in 1923, Hitler launched his unsuccessful Beer Hall Putsch in Munich, and precisely a decade and half after that, in 1938, synagogues and other Jewish property were destroyed across Germany during the so-called Night of Broken Glass. The three events were intimately related, in terms of timing. The fourth, another major political turning point, was not: the breaching of the Berlin Wall just over a half century later, on November 9, 1989.

That evening, a high-level East German official demonstrated how individual actions and larger, amorphous "structures" can work hand in hand to change the course of history. In response to a question at a press conference in East Berlin, Günter Schabowski of the SED Central Committee misleadingly suggested that a new law allowing for unrestricted travel to the West had gone into effect "right away, immediately."[1] He had misspoken, but news quickly spread that the borders were now open, and thousands of

East Germans descended upon the crossing points in Berlin, demanding passage to the western half of the divided city.

The shocked and confused guards eventually relented, and an initial stream quickly turned into a flood. Schabowski's unwitting "speech act" had opened the Wall by mistake. Thousands of East Germans, jammed into their sputtering Trabis, now flowed into West Berlin, greeted by jubilant crowds on the other side of the Wall. Border guards looked on helplessly, too, as euphoric youths climbed atop the parapets to celebrate. After almost three decades, *the* symbol of Germany division had come toppling down, more with a whimper than a bang.

Communism Crumbles

Unexpected, to be sure, but this sudden turn of world-historical events had not appeared out of nowhere. Historians will long debate the long- and short-term causes of communism's collapse in East Germany, but there is one thing they will surely agree on: the role played by the "Gorbi factor." The Soviet leader's reforms at home, his public renunciation of the use of force, and his insistence that every country could choose its own path were all pivotal. But there was an even larger historical context, of course: Ostpolitik, détente, and the Helsinki Accords, which encouraged dissident movements in Eastern Europe to hold their governments to standards they had publicly (if grudgingly) embraced; the subsequent rise of Solidarity in Poland; as well as political sclerosis and a deteriorating economic situation in the entire Soviet bloc.

In terms of immediate triggers, it all began with Poland and Hungary. By the spring and summer of 1989, "roundtable" discussions with the political opposition had paved the way there to free and fair elections, which quietly upended the communist regimes in both countries and replaced them with democratic forms of government. This had important knock-on effects. That May, just weeks before the Federal Republic celebrated its fortieth anniversary, Hungarian officials began dismantling the barbed-wire barrier to neighboring Austria – the first tear in the Iron Curtain. Word quickly spread, and thousands of East Germans began flowing into Hungary.

The floodgates had opened. But it was not just mass migration to the West, reminiscent of the 1950s crisis that had led to the construction of the Wall, that destabilized the East German regime this time. There was also a great deal of ferment back home. Five days after the opening of the Hungarian border in early May, local elections took place in the GDR. Emboldened by developments elsewhere in the Soviet bloc, East German dissidents carefully monitored the voting process for signs of fraud and manipulation – a normal practice in the GDR, where, according to official statistics, the regime's slate of candidates almost always received upwards of 98 percent of the vote.

It was no surprise that observers detected serious irregularities, but there was one difference this time. Local citizens' groups protested the results by publicly calling out the regime – an especially courageous act, considering developments elsewhere in the communist world at the time. On June 4, Chinese authorities brutally put down a student protest movement that had gathered since mid-April in Beijing's Tiananmen Square.

Top East German officials publicly came out in support of the Chinese crackdown, a clear warning signal to dissidents at home. But this did not deter critics of the regime, especially in major urban centers like the Saxon city of Leipzig, where, since the early 1980s, they had found sanctuary in the local Lutheran church. Starting that fall, large weekly protests took place there every Monday following a solemn prayer for peace. The numbers really exploded in early October, just as officials were festively celebrating the GDR's fortieth anniversary on October 7.

The turning point came two days later, when tens of thousands turned out for that week's Monday demonstration in Leipzig, chanting, "*We* are the people!" and "No violence!" – a plea *and* an allusion to recent events in China. Rumors swirled that authorities were indeed planning to use force, that they were even stockpiling extra blood for transfusions in local hospitals. In the end, the protest and the regime's response remained peaceful, thanks in no small part to joint efforts by local party officials and Kurt Masur, the famous conductor of the Leipzig Gewandhaus Orchestra, who encouraged both sides to refrain from violence.

The SED had blinked, and demonstrations attracting hundreds of thousands of protesters now spread across the entire country. Grassroots opposition groups, with names like New Forum and Democracy Now, also began forming that fall. They issued urgent calls for democratic elections and demanded basic freedoms, including an end to censorship and one-party rule, as well as the right to travel abroad without restrictions. Erich Honecker resigned on October 18, only to be replaced by another hardliner, Egon Krenz.

The "peaceful revolution" reached its highpoint on November 4, when a half million ordinary East Germans gathered for a demonstration in the center of East Berlin, where they heard fiery, sometimes moving speeches by leading dissidents, critical artists and intellectuals, as well as a handful of remorseful SED officials. Five days later, the Berlin Wall fell, and on December 3, Krenz and the entire Politburo resigned. Paralyzed by mass emigration, large-scale protest at home, and an economic crisis of its own doing, the SED regime had come to an ignominious end.

The Rocky Road to Unity

That did not necessarily mean the GDR would soon cease to exist as well. The new opposition groups were, for starters, opposed to some sort of unification with West Germany. They hoped instead to introduce a reformed, democratic version of socialism – something that may have had to do with lingering feelings of resentment. After all, they had largely been ignored by visiting West German dignitaries who, hoping to maintain a mini-détente in the midst of a renascent Cold War, had cozied up instead to regime representatives in the 1980s.

Despite the general sense of euphoria in the Federal Republic, there were also voices there that were less than enthusiastic about any sort of union between the two states – even though the Basic Law of 1949 explicitly called for the "unity and freedom" of Germany as a whole. The Green Party emphatically rejected unification, with one prominent member calling it "historically obsolete."[2] A handful of prominent Social Democrats were also opposed. This included Minister President Oskar Lafontaine of the Saarland, an outlier among the old and new elites in his party who would nevertheless be chosen to run against Helmut Kohl as the SPD candidate for chancellor in the winter of 1990.

A number of economists issued similar warnings about unifying too rapidly, especially after shocking revelations detailing the extent of economic damage in the GDR. Foreign leaders also expressed serious misgivings, including West Germany's closest allies, above all France's François Mitterrand and Margaret Thatcher in the UK. Kohl's well-known commitment to European integration certainly helped ease their apprehensions but concerns about the perennial German Question were clearly alive and well.

The mood had quickly shifted in East Germany itself, where a groundswell of popular support for unification emerged shortly after the fall of the Wall. The slogan "We are *one* people" abruptly replaced "We are *the* people" in mid-November in Leipzig, the epicenter of the "peaceful revolution" – to the chagrin of those who had led the opposition movement earlier that fall. But their voices were quickly drowned out. On November 28, Helmut Kohl surprised the world by presenting to the Bundestag a Ten-Point Plan for German Unity, which emphasized the importance of national self-determination. At the same time, by calling for a slow, gradual process – an approach that quickly fell to the wayside – Kohl sought to assuage the fears of Germany's allies and neighbors on both sides of the Cold War divide. The German Question was indeed back on the "agenda of world history."[3]

There was pushback, to be sure, but in the end, the factors allowing for unification outweighed those militating against it. For one, Kohl and Foreign Minister Hans-Dietrich Genscher sniffed a historic opportunity and decided to take advantage of it before it was too late – not unlike those East Germans who had fled en masse to the West in the spring, summer, and fall of 1989. After all, no one knew how long Gorbachev would remain in power. As an attempted Soviet military coup in August 1991 later bore out, that was no idle consideration.

There were others. Because migration to the West continued unabated, especially on the part of the young and educated, there was increasing pressure to make it more palatable to remain in the East, where the economic situation looked increasingly bleak. Besides, some argued, whatever the economic risks of unification, it was unfair that the burden of World War II had fallen so unevenly for forty years on the shoulders of those living in the East. In the end, West Germany's economic might made unification both conceivable and feasible.

Elections held in the GDR in mid-March 1990 decided the matter – at least on the domestic side. A dozen parties entered the field, including the SPD and former "bloc parties" like the CDU, which had merged with their counterparts in the West after decades of subjugation to the SED. In mid-December, the East German ruling party ceased to exist – at least in name. Under Gregor Gysi, a charismatic young attorney who had made a name for himself in the GDR by representing prominent dissidents, the SED refounded itself in early February under a new moniker, the Party of Democratic Socialism (PDS).

This "rebranding" accomplished two important goals: it created distance to the SED while ensuring that the new party inherited its predecessor's considerable finances. The gamble paid off, and the PDS managed to win more than 16 percent of the vote. In a less successful strategic move, the opposition movements that had formed that fall merged into a new party, Alliance 90 (*Bündnis 90*) – to no avail. They received less than 3 percent of the vote, a clear statement about their unpopular but principled opposition to unification.

The big winner was the conservative CDU, which received more than 40 percent – nearly twice as much as the next strongest party, the SPD. Small wonder, given Oskar Lafontaine's skepticism about unification *and* Kohl's announcement, a month earlier, of plans for a currency union between East and West Germany. This was to take effect on July 1, giving East Germans immediate access to the coveted deutschmark. Disdainful critics accused the East German "masses" of succumbing to base material interests. But for West Germans who had long enjoyed comfort and prosperity, or for East German artists and intellectuals who had "loftier" concerns and interests, it was easy to be critical of more mundane desires, like the wish to buy a video recorder or go on vacation in Mallorca. Besides, most East Germans seemed receptive to democracy and the rule of law, even if few had ever experienced them personally – and even if their commitment to those ideals would be questioned repeatedly in the coming decades.

One should not forget, in this context, that most West Germans had not exactly been dyed-in-the-wool democrats in the first decades after World War II. One wonders, moreover, how attached they would have remained to democracy in the absence of sustained material prosperity starting in the 1950s. In any event, it was not *just* about money and material possessions for most "Ossis," as East Germans were now (for the most part, affectionately) called – and the overwhelming majority had spoken clearly in favor of unification.

Some of the same individuals who looked down on "venal" motivations also called into question the very nature of the upheaval. It was not a "real" revolution, they suggested, because it did not create anything "new" but merely "caught up" with what the West had already achieved – mirroring, in a sense, the fallen regime's own earlier efforts to play catch-up with the West.[4] The largely peaceful manner in which the SED dictatorship was overthrown also made the events of 1989–90 seem somehow suspect. How could there be a "real" revolution in the absence of blood and violence, careful planning and organization?

Such claims unfairly downplay the courage of those who took to the streets, given the very real possibility of physical force – especially with Tiananmen Square fresh in most minds. They also ignore those instances in which the regime, and some protesters, did indeed resort to strong-arm measures that fall. In the end, it is fair to say that (East) Germany's fate was largely decided in the streets.[5]

There has also been some debate about the actual causes leading to the downfall and collapse of the GDR. Was it the result of the hardline policies favored by politicians like Konrad Adenauer and later Ronald Reagan, who ratcheted up the nuclear arms race and famously called on Gorbachev to "tear down this Wall" during a visit to West Berlin in June 1987?[6] Or was it the result of Ostpolitik and détente, that is, of policies that had sought to bring about change by improving living standards in the East, to undermine the regime by establishing greater human contact across the Iron Curtain?

Good arguments can be made for both approaches, in hindsight. The arms race of the 1980s made it increasingly difficult for the USSR to remain solvent and introduce necessary reforms. But the opening to the West had equally important repercussions. Dissident movements flourished in the wake of Helsinki, as did consumption of Western media and consumer goods. After 1975, East German authorities turned a blind eye to those who clandestinely listened to or watched West German radio and television – quite a switch from the early 1960s, when members of the Free German Youth organization had climbed onto rooftops to dismantle antennae directed toward the West.

At the same time, greater access to coveted Western goods and greater exposure to life in the Federal Republic – with its fast cars and overflowing shops – heightened expectations that were ultimately frustrated, as the GDR sank deeper and deeper into debt. The regime simply proved unable to satisfy everyday demands and find workable solutions to intractable problems. This was a classic instance of the so-called Tocqueville effect or paradox. "The most dangerous time for a bad government," the nineteenth-century

French sociologist Alexis de Tocqueville contended, is "usually when it begins to reform" but then fails to make good on its promises. This destabilizes an unloved regime by instigating a "revolution of rising expectations" – precisely, one could argue, what happened in the GDR in the 1980s.[7] In the end, improved consumption and small liberties were not enough to stave off communism's collapse; in fact, they likely hastened it.

Two Plus Four Equals One

Whatever the reasons for the downfall of state socialism, the move toward unification continued apace after Kohl's announcement on November 28. Konrad Adenauer's staunch commitment to the West decades earlier and Willy Brandt's subsequent overtures to the East had not only made this possible but also ensured its peaceful character. There were nevertheless a few major sticking points along the way. Would unified Germany be allowed to join NATO? Would it formally recognize the Oder–Neisse border separating the country from Poland since 1945? Would the Germans finally pay reparations to East Europeans who had been forced to work as slave laborers during the Third Reich? These were touchy subjects that prompted tenacious debate and gave rise to fierce negotiations.

For understandable reasons, Moscow opposed, whereas Bonn and Washington both insisted on, German membership in NATO. And despite the concessions made by his predecessor Willy Brandt two decades earlier at the height of Ostpolitik, Kohl was wary of formally renouncing large swathes of territory in the East that had belonged to Germany for hundreds of years – not least for fear of alienating the expellee organizations that still enjoyed a powerful lobbying position in his party.

In the end, a compromise was found that more or less linked these issues and elicited concessions from all sides. Kohl caved on the border in return for a Polish promise to drop their insistence on reparations; he also agreed to negotiate a separate treaty to compensate former slave laborers (*Ostarbeiter*) excluded from any form of compensation after World War II. Gorbachev, for his part, yielded on NATO membership in return for an alleged promise that no foreign troops or nuclear weapons would ever be stationed on the territory of the former GDR.[8] But that was not all. To sweeten the deal, the chancellor promised substantial financial assistance to the USSR, which was experiencing a severe debt crisis and crippling food shortages at the time.

In essence, the Federal Republic purchased political concessions, and its robust economy allowed it to do so. But personal connections also played a role here. Despite early misgivings about the new Soviet premier, whom he had compared once to Nazi propaganda chief Joseph Goebbels, Chancellor Kohl developed a good working relationship with Gorbachev, and a series of meetings between the two leaders in the summer of 1990 paved the way for the so-called Two Plus Four Treaty, a major international agreement that incorporated the various compromises.[9] Signed that September by the two German states and the four victorious powers of World War II, it formally ended that bloody conflict – forty-five years after the fact – and paved the path to German unification.

The *practical* process of unifying the two German states was a source of further debate, this time on the domestic front. The drafters of West Germany's Basic Law had intended the document to be a provisional one, that is, until a properly "reunified" German people could adopt a new constitution. This was clearly set forth in Article 46, and representatives of East Germany's main political groupings – both dissidents *and* reform communists – even drafted a new constitution in the early months of 1990. In the end, their work as members of the Central Round Table, a discussion forum charged with proposing political reforms for the GDR, was for naught. According to a different section of the Basic Law, Article 23, other German states had the right to join ("accede to") the Federal Republic, if they so desired – and that was ultimately what would take place. Helmut Kohl threw his considerable weight behind this speedier and seemingly more efficient solution. Besides, the chancellor and others argued, why fix something that was not broken?

This gave rise to a great deal of criticism, especially on the Left, where many had hoped to salvage the supposedly more sanguine aspects of state socialism: a constitutionally guaranteed "right to work," for example, more liberal abortion and contraception laws, and, last but not least, generous social welfare policies that made it easier for women to enter the labor force. Others argued that the transfer of West German legal and especially economic structures to the other side of the Elbe should take place at a much slower pace, instead of throwing East Germans into the proverbial deep end. Such arguments cost Oskar Lafontaine the chancellorship in December 1990, when unified Germany's first federal elections took place. But, in hindsight, his skepticism about the high costs of unification was not entirely off the mark.

The conservative CDU/CSU were the big winners of that election. The PDS also performed well, thanks to a one-time modification of German electoral law, which allowed parties to enter the Bundestag *if* they were based in the East *and* received at least 5 percent of the vote there. The Greens, for their part, failed to clear the 5-percent hurdle, and the SPD experienced its worst thrashing since 1957.

"Blooming Landscapes"

At first, it seemed that the naysayers had received their just desserts. But after a two-year honeymoon made possible by an economic boom stimulated by construction and public works projects, the Eastern economy began to fall apart. Its industry essentially collapsed, leading to crippling levels of unemployment, a phenomenon practically unknown there under state socialism. Some sectors, like agriculture and mining, were hit worse than others, as were certain age groups. Those in their forties and fifties suffered most: too young to retire and, it was thought, too old to be retrained. More than a million East Germans – one-tenth of those who had been employed in 1989 – were out of work by the mid-1990s, and another 2 million found themselves in early retirement or working "short-time."

There were a number of reasons for this precipitous economic decline. For starters, East German industry was unable to compete on the world market. The currency reform had made its goods much too expensive, especially given their reputation for inferior quality. Trade with former allies in the Soviet bloc collapsed as well, and most East Germans preferred to purchase Western-made products, long desired and long associated with excellence.

Continuing emigration to the West, as well as the legacy of state socialism – run-down factories and plants, poor infrastructure, low productivity, and catastrophic environmental degradation – all played a role as well. As a result, approximately half of all firms and enterprises were working at a loss, and some regions became ghost towns, especially in places where the local economy had been closely tied to the fate of a single, now defunct, factory or industry. In short, the sort of "deindustrialization" familiar to northern

England and the American rustbelt set in across the former GDR.

All of this was doubly disappointing, given the optimistic promises made during the lead-up to the December 1990 election. In contrast to Lafontaine's economic pessimism, Helmut Kohl (in)famously spoke of "blooming landscapes" on the horizon in the East, promising further that "no one will be worse off than before, but many better off."[10] The chancellor was not just trying to win an election; he was also hoping to stanch the flow of East Germans to the West, which was impeding the "transformation" of the East into a capitalist, market economy.

Still, his overly optimistic promises inflated expectations that would soon be bitterly disappointed. Another pledge was that unification could be financed without a tax increase, but rather through sustained economic growth. Such promises were not completely disingenuous, given the impressive strength of the West German economy at the time. But in the end, the cheerful prognoses did not pan out.

Consider the fate of *Treuhand*, a government agency ("trust") responsible for restructuring and privatizing the thousands of state-owned enterprises spread across the GDR. German authorities anticipated that Treuhand would make a fortune – but then cut its legs out from under it by adopting the principle of "restitution before compensation." What this meant was that property that had been expropriated under the communist regime would be given back to its original owners instead of offering them compensation for their earlier loss. There was much to be said for this approach, but it ultimately scared off potential investors and buyers by creating a great deal of uncertainty about ownership rights. Instead of making money to help finance unification, Treuhand wound up amassing some 300 billion deutschmarks in debt by the time it ceased operations in 1994.

By that point, the agency had privatized (or reprivatized) two thirds of the more than 12,000 enterprises placed under its control, often at dirt-cheap prices. It simply shut down another third, and that mass liquidation (*Abwicklung*) came to symbolize for many "Ossis" the supposed "sellout" of the East – in more than one sense of the word. By throwing millions of East Germans out of work, Treuhand did not just contribute to high levels of unemployment. Its actions left a bad taste that severely hurt the image of the entire unification process, and it quickly became the bogeyman of the entire economic "transformation" of the East.

That was understandable but not entirely fair. After all, the agency had simply served as the "messenger," revealing the culprit ultimately responsible for all these difficulties, namely, the decrepit state of the GDR economy. At the same time, it helped create a viable, if much smaller, industrial core in the East by cutting away the "fat." Small consolation, of course, to the millions who lost their jobs as a result.

How, in the end, *did* the Germans cover the outsized costs of unification and find money for massive subsidies, economic restructuring, and the currency union; the introduction of modern infrastructure and communications; as well as environmental clean-up in the hardest hit industrial regions and cities, such as Bitterfeld, which quickly became synonymous with East German ecological degradation? Despite solemn promises not to raise taxes, the government introduced a so-called solidarity supplement (*Solidaritätszuschlag*) in early 1991 – a throwback to the Equalization of Burdens Law of 1952 (see p. 48). In essence, this was a surtax on income and capital gains, earmarked specifically for unification. The costs were also covered by a substantial hike in social security premiums, as well as massive borrowing, which eventually resulted in a doubling of the national debt. By the end of the 1990s, the price of unification had exceeded more than a trillion deutschmarks.

Unification and its Discontents

No surprise, then, that unification caused a great deal of anger and resentment – but not primarily on the part of those who footed the bill. To be sure, the initial euphoria that greeted the fall of the Wall – the word *awesome* (*Wahnsinn*) was on many lips in the days and weeks following November 9, 1989 – soon gave way to resentment: for example, about the throngs of East Germans (and other Eastern Europeans) who flocked to West Berlin and the Federal Republic to buy up coveted Western products like video recorders. Their penchant for bananas, another rare commodity in the GDR, was the source of many mean-spirited jokes. Yet, it was ultimately those born and raised in the GDR who would become most disgruntled – even if their lot compared favorably overall to that of those who had lived in the other former Soviet-bloc countries. But once again, that was not their point of comparison. West Germany was.

There were many reasons for East German anger – among them frequently disdainful treatment by the many "arrogant" and judgmental West Germans suspicious about widespread xenophobia and a supposed lack of commitment to democracy in the "spy-infested" East. Socialism had supposedly "warped" East Germans in other ways as well, making them "lazy," "unproductive," and far "too dependent" on state handouts. The feeling of resentment was mutual, and many "Ossis" were equally scornful of "superficial" West German "materialism" and of "dog-eat-dog" capitalism more generally – the same type of knee-jerk criticism, incidentally, many leftist West Germans had long made about Americans. They considered themselves, by contrast, to be more "down-to-earth," "socially minded," and "solidary."

Forty years apart and socialized in radically different ways under a different political system: that surely left a mark. How could it have been otherwise? Still, there was no shortage of tired clichés on either side of the former German–German border. Greater tact, empathy, and understanding for what East

Germans had experienced – for the fact that *they* were the Germans who had suffered most and longest for Hitler's genocidal war – might have gone a long way in reducing their sense of resentment and insecurity as "second-class" Germans. A franker, more realistic assessment on high of the coming challenges would have helped as well.

In any event, the "blooming landscapes" promised by Helmut Kohl remained fallow for a long time, and that was no doubt the greatest source of disappointment. Some cities and urban regions did flourish, to be sure: Dresden and Leipzig, (East) Berlin and Jena, the headquarters of the world-renowned Zeiss optical firm. Other areas fared less well, especially rural regions, which young people left in droves. Crippling levels of unemployment were, understandably, the greatest source of anger. Income and wealth also remained noticeably lower in the East, though the cost of living tended to be lower there as well. The impression that the West had "colonized" or "annexed" the East – embodied in the large numbers of West Germans who descended on the territory of the former GDR to take up high-level jobs in government, civil service, and universities – was another source of anger. Easterners were disproportionately underrepresented in leadership positions, a disheartening trend that continues – and continues to raise ire – today.[11]

Melancholy, disappointment, and a distinct sense of being somehow unfairly disadvantaged were the lot of many East Germans. Not all. There were clearly some "winners," though their voices tended to get drowned out in the cacophony of complaints. Pensioners, for instance, enjoyed much higher incomes than they would have received under state socialism, where many had been forced to work beyond retirement age to make ends meet. Immense construction projects dotted the landscape and helped drive the initial economic boom. Easterners also benefitted from the introduction of the most modern transportation and communications systems – much as West Germans had benefitted from the introduction of modern factories and infrastructure after 1945, to make up for wartime destruction. The successful transfer of democratic institutions, efficient administrative structures, and the rule of law were, of course, also nothing to sneeze at.

Not all was doom and gloom, then, and the economic disparities gradually diminished. If this process took decades longer than anticipated (and promised), this had much to do with the miserable economic legacy of state socialism. Besides, regional differences were nothing new. Beginning in the 1960s, West Germany's southern states, like Bavaria and Baden-Württemberg, had begun to surpass their northern neighbors in terms of wealth and general living standards. This was overshadowed by the East–West "gap" after 1989, but over time, differences among some of the old federal states (*Länder*) – say, between wealthy Hamburg and the ailing industrial Ruhr region – were the same or even greater than those between East and West. Unemployment levels were certainly comparable to those in the East in some "deindustrialized" Western regions.

Still, discernible differences remained. Those living on the territory of the former GDR tended to be more secular, a legacy of the SED's antipathy toward organized religion. They were also less civically engaged, as a rule, yet another legacy of state socialism – just as reports in the early 1960s of low levels of "civic culture" in West Germany had been a partial product of Nazi-era socialization.[12]

Foreign Policy and the Return of the German Question

Overcoming those differences and creating "Germans" out of "Ossis" and "Wessis" signaled, in a sense, a return to the original German Question: how to forge political, socioeconomic, and cultural unity among ethnic Germans who hailed from different regions and had dissimilar historical experiences? This had been one of Bismarck's most challenging tasks after unification in 1871, and the Iron Chancellor accomplished this, in part, by creating pariah groups: socialists, Catholics, and other alleged "enemies of the empire." German conservatives flirted with a similar strategy after 1990, dismissively referring to the PDS and its supporters as dyed-in-the-wool "red socks" (*Rote Socken*, or "lefties").

Demolishing the metaphorical "walls in the head" that had replaced the concrete Wall dividing East and West Germans is a continuing process, even today. But it was not the only "German Question" that resurfaced after the unexpected collapse of communism. Unification gave rise to a great deal of anguish and handwringing at the time in a different sense. Would unified Germany remain a "tamed power," or would the country revert to its dangerous and destructive ways of yore and pose a threat to its neighbors once again? Had the country truly "learned the lessons" of its history?[13]

Doomsayers at home and abroad feared that a newly aggressive Germany was looming on the horizon. Concerns that the hoary German Question was about to return with a vengeance turned out to be largely unwarranted, for the "new" Federal Republic remained committed to the same core principles that had guided its foreign policy since the 1950s: predictability and self-restraint, reliability and a commitment to working together with others in a multilateral framework. There were nevertheless some shifts, and they quickly became apparent when the post-Cold War "peace dividend" proved short-lived and a number of international crises erupted in the early 1990s – starting with the first Gulf War, which began just months after the two German states unified.

Despite pressure from its allies to participate militarily in the fight to liberate Kuwait from Iraq, the Federal Republic limited its involvement to logistical support. This included the deployment of minesweepers to the Persian Gulf. It also contributed billions of deutschmarks to the war effort, a response that critics contemptuously characterized as "checkbook diplomacy." But the German government refused to send combat troops, justifying its decision on constitutional grounds. The Basic Law, the argument went, limited the use of Germany's armed force to "purposes of defense" and could not be deployed "out-of-area," that is, beyond NATO territory.

But that was not the only reason. Nowhere else in the West was public opposition to the American-led war effort as vigorous as it was in Germany. Large-scale protests took place across the Federal Republic, frequently tinged by the sort of anti-Americanism typical of leftist protest in West Germany since the 1960s. There was also widespread criticism, at home and abroad, of German firms that had sold chemical weapons to Saddam Hussein, who began launching so-called Scud missiles against Israel in January 1991. This only fueled careless comparisons that some Western leaders were publicly making between the Iraqi leader and Adolf Hitler. But it was also why some on the political Left – including the former East German dissident Wolf Biermann, whose father had died at Auschwitz – vigorously came out in support of the war.[14]

Foreign criticism of unified Germany's steadfast refusal to participate militarily in Operation Desert Storm elicited a great deal of criticism from the country's allies – creating, in a sense, a new twist on the old German Question. Was the country now pursuing a different kind of "special path": a pacifist one, foreign critics complained, that unchivalrously left its allies in the lurch? "First the Germans were accused of not taking off their combat boots," a frustrated Helmut Kohl quipped, "and now they are accused of not putting them on."[15]

The darker aspects of Germany's recent past came to the fore in these debates, especially at home, where opinions divided sharply over what their country's international role in the new, post-Cold War world should be. The unspeakable suffering caused and experienced by Germans during World War II had produced a robust aversion to militarism and highly ambivalent feelings about the use of force – also in the East, where there had been widespread criticism of conscription and paramilitary activities. Pacifism was something most Germans had in common, and, for this reason, they took pride in the Federal Republic's vaunted "culture of restraint," a catchphrase that neatly captured the country's steadfast rejection of old-style power politics, reluctance to resort to force, and firm refusal to project power and throw its weight around aggressively – at least when it came to military action. As Willy Brandt once dryly observed, "There are worse things than pacifist Germans."[16]

Other prominent politicians, for their part, called for Germany to assume a more active role on the world stage. The restoration of full sovereignty following unification meant that their country now had greater responsibilities in the international arena, they argued, including ones involving the use of military force. But there was a flip side to all this. It also meant that Germany now had greater freedom to say "nein." Questions about its "proper" role on the world stage first sparked debate during the Gulf War but became especially contentious during the next major international crisis: the bloody dissolution of Yugoslavia, which led to the first military conflict in Europe since World War II, just months after the defeat of Saddam Hussein.

The wars that took place in the Balkans in the 1990s helped to clarify and shape the country's new international role, but things did not go well at the outset. West European efforts to end hostilities failed, in no small part, thanks to the actions of German foreign minister Hans-Dietrich Genscher. Fighting began when Croatia and Slovenia – angered about Serbia's dominance in the Southern Slav federation, as well as the increasingly rabid nationalist rhetoric emanating from Belgrade – decided to secede from Yugoslavia in June 1991. Genscher not only insisted on recognizing their independence but also exerted considerable pressure on the West European allies to follow suit, ostensibly in the hope that that this would contain Serb aggression and nip the conflict in the bud. Foreign critics suspected a different reason, namely, that Germany was trying to reassert the dominant economic position it had enjoyed in the region before World War II. Whatever Genscher's motives, his actions became a source of vigorous debate and controversy, with detractors at home and abroad blaming him for the deteriorating situation in the Balkans.

A new conflict began there in the spring of 1992, when Bosnia-Herzegovina also declared its independence. This sparked a more brutal, more protracted struggle involving mass killings, "ethnic cleansing," large-scale rape, as well as incarceration in detention facilities that were referred to as "concentration camps" – a term that resonated strongly in the Federal Republic, for obvious reasons. Germans, other Europeans, and the rest of the world looked on helplessly for three years, unwilling to intervene militarily and unable to devise an effective nonmilitary response. It was only after a genocidal massacre took place in July 1995 in the Bosnian town of Srebrenica – the worst war crime in Europe in a half century – that NATO, led by the United States, took decisive military action, with air strikes finally bringing the Serbs to the negotiating table. The Dayton Peace Agreement, brokered by American officials, was signed in the late fall of 1995.

Germany's response to these conflicts, first in the Gulf region and then the Balkans, laid bare the foreign policy challenges and dilemmas it now faced in the wake of unification. What *was* its "proper" role on the world stage, given that the Europeans, seemingly incapable of devising a common foreign policy, remained dependent on American leadership? Could

German military force be used for missions that went beyond defensive purposes and took place "out-of-area," that is, outside of NATO territory? If so, would that require a constitutional amendment – so soon after West German leaders had staunchly refused to make any such changes when absorbing the GDR?

The shadow of recent German history loomed large in these debates. But the legacy and lessons of the Third Reich and the Holocaust were not at all clearcut. In fact, Germany's expansionist, genocidal past was used to draw diametrically opposed conclusions about the country's "appropriate" role in the world. Those who tended to see Germany's hands tied because of its history, who spoke passionately of a "duty to nonviolence" because of Nazi atrocities, met with equally heartfelt counterarguments by those who pointed to their country's past as an injunction to act. "We have a political and moral duty to assist, precisely *in light of* our history," Germany's top diplomat told colleagues in June 1995, just two weeks before the genocidal massacre at Srebrenica. "It was, after all, the Allies who – using military force, by the way – freed us from the Nazi dictatorship. . . ."[17]

Two popular slogans – "Never again Auschwitz" and "Never again war" – encapsulated the harrowing dilemma Germans faced. They also demonstrated just how ambivalent the burden of history could be. Participating in international military interventions intended to stop mass slaughter and foreign aggression was not the same as waging an expansionist war, of course. Still, in the case of Bosnia, the Wehrmacht's notorious role in the Balkans during World War II made the issue far from clearcut. The Constitutional Court in Karlsruhe finally decided the matter in a landmark ruling announced in July 1994. "Out-of-area" missions were indeed permissible *if* conducted under the aegis of a "mutual collective security" system – such as NATO – and *if* the Bundestag approved.[18] The Federal Republic did not send combat troops to Bosnia, but it did perform aerial reconnaissance during the war and joined the UN's peacekeeping mission after the signing of the Dayton Peace Agreement.

This marked an important sea change in the realm of foreign affairs. The clearest shift was a new if unenthusiastic willingness to use military force to resolve violent conflicts and achieve humanitarian goals in foreign lands – though never unilaterally, only after much soul-searching, almost always under pressure from abroad, and without fail as part of an international peacekeeping or humanitarian mission. Since 1991, the Federal Republic has participated in dozens of these and deployed more than 100,000 soldiers abroad – from Southeast Asia to Southeastern Europe, from Central Africa to the Middle East. As we shall see in the next chapter, the most important milestone came in March 1999, with German participation in the NATO-led Kosovo War – the first time German soldiers had engaged in actual combat since 1945.

Military missions beyond NATO territory would have been well-nigh "unthinkable" before the fall of the Berlin Wall. Increasingly bold, piecemeal deployments became gradually more acceptable. But because of old mindsets, they remained far from routine. Germany nevertheless remained a reliable partner, on the whole. At the same time, its leaders displayed a noticeable increase in self-confidence and a greater willingness to assert its independence – now that the Cold War was over, the threat of nuclear annihilation had receded, and unification had finally been achieved. This gave the country greater room for maneuver, allowing it to be more self-assertive *and* more interventionist. Germany's controversial role in the recognition of Croatia and Slovenia in the winter of 1991, its (unsuccessful) bid a few years later to gain a permanent seat on the UN Security Council, and its participation in international deployments to Bosnia and other trouble spots, like Cambodia and Somalia, were all prominent examples of this.

Unified Germany proved, in short, that it was willing to assume greater global responsibilities in the post-Wall world. And whatever fears its neighbors and domestic critics may have initially harbored, it did not become a trigger-happy, expansionist player with "great power" aspirations – just the opposite, in fact, and that was encouraging. But there were other, less reassuring developments in Germany in the wake of unification – none more disturbing than the rise of violent xenophobia, which seriously damaged the country's reputation abroad.

"Coming to Terms" with the Past – and with Xenophobia in the Present

A series of brutal racist attacks, including pogrom-like "hunts" for foreigners and the use of Molotov cocktails to destroy their homes, took place soon after unification – casting a pall on that otherwise joyful event. By 1993, almost fifty foreigners had been killed, including children. This took place on *both* sides of the Elbe, even though many had the impression that xenophobic violence was far worse in the East. It certainly was disproportionately higher there, in terms of population density, but the rise of a radical right-wing scene was not limited to half the newly unified country – though it had been kept in check, more or less, under the SED.

There were a number of reasons for the uptick in racist violence, the worst in Germany since 1945. This included a huge surge in the number of refugees and asylum-seekers, starting in the late 1970s but even more so after the end of the Cold War. That increase stoked concerns about letting in "too many" foreigners, especially "bogus" ones supposedly coming to Germany to take advantage of the Federal Republic's generous social welfare policies.

Xenophobic sentiment was greatest among those Germans who were less well off, felt they had few prospects, or feared social decline – just as Hitler's venomous antisemitism had appealed to the hardest hit during the Great Depression. But it also became increasingly and more openly acceptable among nationalist and conservative intellectuals, journalists, and other elites, the so-called New Right, who vigorously denied that Germany was an "immigration country." Rehashing Helmut Kohl's calls in the 1980s for greater national "self-confidence," they worried that a large influx of foreigners would negatively affect German "identity" and "culture." Mainstream conservatives harbored similar concerns and successfully pushed for a reform of Germany's liberal approach to political asylum. In mid-1993, a constitutional amendment made it more difficult for foreigners to seek refuge in the Federal Republic, and the number of applicants dropped precipitously.

Did this mean that Germany was backsliding, that its vaunted "culture of remembrance" had been a short-lived sham – that Germans were no longer the "world champions" of "coming to terms" with the past? No. Large-scale protests and candle-light vigils against assorted xenophobic outrages cast doubt on any notion that Germans, as a whole, were reverting once again into Nazis. It was primarily, but not solely, young people in urban centers who attended those demonstrations – the same young people, incidentally, who tended to rally behind political scientist Daniel J. Goldhagen, whose controversial book, *Hitler's Willing Executioners*, became a bestseller in the spring of 1996.[19] Most academics and public intellectuals rejected the young American's theory that a special form of "eliminationist antisemitism" peculiar to Germany had been at the root of the Holocaust. Instead of denying what some critics dismissed as a return to the notion of "collective guilt" for Nazi crimes, younger Germans seemed at pains to condemn and thereby distance themselves from their country's awful past by embracing Goldhagen's tendentious arguments.

Whatever their reasons, the "Goldhagen debate" was one of several major controversies about Germany's dark history that dominated public discussion in the mid-1990s. Others included the decision to construct a large memorial in the center of Berlin – the capital of unified Germany once again – to commemorate the Nazi genocide of Europe's Jews; monetary compensation for East European slave laborers and Jews from the region who had been excluded from previous payments; the role of Swiss banks during the Holocaust; and, last but not least, the so-called Wehrmacht Exhibition, which traveled across Germany starting in March 1995.

That controversial show, which focused on Wehrmacht crimes in the 1940s, challenged the still popular myth that ordinary German soldiers had conducted a "clean" and "honorable" war in the East. This provoked a great deal of vituperative pushback, especially by German veterans. Others, like the respected novelist Martin Walser, later delivered a controversial and much commented on speech that decried the supposed instrumentalization of German memory politics, provocatively calling ubiquitous invocations of the Holocaust a "moral cudgel."[20]

These debates made clear just how much popular interest and scholarly controversy the Third Reich and the Final Solution continued to attract after unification. But the focus was not just on Germans as perpetrators. The 1990s also witnessed a noticeable uptick in public and scholarly discussion about Germans as victims. The focus was on aerial bombardment by the Allies during World War II and the mass expulsion of millions of ethnic Germans from Eastern Europe during and right after the war. In short, the decade following the fall of the Wall witnessed the postwar period's most sustained and intense public discussion of the atrocities perpetrated during the Third Reich – despite competition from a new source of memory and "memory politics," namely, *communist* crimes committed after 1945.

Starting with the storming of the headquarters of the Ministry for State Security in East Berlin in January 1990 – intended to prevent further destruction of the reams of files its agents had assiduously collected on dissidents and other "enemies" of the regime – professional and popular interest in GDR history focused on the regime's repressive apparatus and on especially sordid stories about Stasi surveillance. A feverish and often sensational search for former informers, often with little regard for the exact nature of their collaboration with the regime, seemed to be a belated attempt to make up for inadequate denazification after 1945. Trials and investigations of those considered most complicit – border guards,

Stasi officials and alleged informers, high-level SED functionaries like Erich Honecker and Egon Krenz – grabbed headlines for several years and resulted in a series of well-publicized controversies, especially when documents were found that seemed to incriminate active politicians originally from the East.

This top-down, politically inflected, often morally accusatory and triumphalist approach to the East German past seemed, at times, to efface the differences between the Third Reich and the GDR. There is no question: both dictatorships were highly repressive and ruined the lives of those deemed dangerous, difficult, or somehow dodgy. But there was an important distinction, as many have pointed out. The Nazis produced mounds of corpses – the Stasi and the SED mounds of documents. At the same time, this approach struck many "Ossis" as arrogant and disdainful, fueling anger, resentment, and what came to be known as *Ostalgie* – an almost defiant "nostalgia" for the supposedly more positive aspects of state socialism. However understandable that reaction may have been, much that was now looked back upon wistfully – such as supposedly high levels of social solidarity under state socialism – had not been *achievements* of the regime but rather responses to its very *deficiencies*. That was a subtle but important distinction.

The Twilight of the Kohl Era

Unified Germany's unswerving commitment to European unity helped allay – and was *intended* to allay – whatever fears some at home and abroad may have had about the rise of a Fourth Reich.[21] Helmut Kohl's staunch support of greater integration played an important role here, even though Europe's other leaders steadfastly rejected his insistent calls since the late 1980s for some form of political unity, fearing it would only cement Germany's dominant position on the continent. The "chancellor of unity" – in more than one sense of the phrase – eventually abandoned his appeals, focusing instead on other ways to expand and intensify the European project.

The most important move here was the signing of a major new treaty in the small Dutch town of Maastricht in early 1992, made possible by the end of the Cold War. Heralded as a "new stage in the process of creating an ever-closer union among the peoples of Europe," the Treaty on European Union foresaw a number of innovations: the creation of a common currency by the close of the millennium, joint foreign and security policies, as well as more powerful and democratic European institutions, including the Parliament in Strasbourg.[22] The newly rechristened European Union (EU) was, in a sense, *the* solution to the German Question.

Kohl's calls for political unity may have fallen on deaf ears, but the Maastricht Treaty certainly contained distinct advantages for the Federal Republic – even if abandoning the mighty deutschmark for a common currency seemed a stiff price to pay to allay fears about unification and German economic predominance. It was nevertheless one that ultimately accrued to the benefit of German exports, as did the opening of EU membership to the markets of Eastern Europe. To make that possible, the treaty established criteria intended to stabilize the new democracies and prop up their economies, with each member – and potential member – pledging to keep inflation rates and budget deficits below certain levels. This was one reason why the Federal Republic subsequently adopted a raft of neoliberal policies: lower taxes, greater deregulation, and (more in theory than practice) cuts in social spending intended to rein in the budget.

Those austerity measures created bad blood, even within the chancellor's own party. One of the most dramatic demonstrations of discontent came in the spring of 1991, when disgruntled East Germans, angry that his campaign promise of "blooming landscapes" had not yet materialized, hurled eggs and insults at Helmut Kohl during a short visit to Halle. The chancellor nevertheless narrowly managed to defeat his colorless opponent, Rudolf Scharping of the SPD, in the 1994 federal elections.

But opposition to his policies only mounted in the following years. The Social Democrats lost the election but maintained control of the Bundesrat, the legislative body that represented the individual German states (*Länder*), and this allowed them to block government efforts to reduce social spending – producing a stagnating state of affairs dubbed "reform gridlock" (*Reformstau*). Organized by the unions and churches, hundreds of thousands of protesters made their frustration known by taking to the streets in the spring of 1996. The increasingly unpopular coalition government seemed incapable of acting, as unemployment soared to almost 10 percent, and the Federal Republic fell behind countries like the United States and Japan in the production of new, cutting-edge technologies. Kohl's days as chancellor seemed to be numbered.

Indeed, his party lost federal elections in the fall of 1998, suffering its worst performance since the founding of the Federal Republic in 1949. In office for just over sixteen years, Helmut Kohl had been the Federal Republic's longest serving chancellor – *and* the head of the first governing coalition whose component parties were both voted out of office. That was not the only novelty of the September 1998 election. For the first time, members of the sixty-eight generation – represented by Gerhard Schröder of the SPD and Joschka Fischer of the Greens – came to power to form postwar Germany's first "Red–Green" coalition. An era had come to an end.

6

Normality? (1998–2024)

According to a scurrilous anecdote from the early 1980s, a relatively young and inebriated Gerhard Schröder stood outside the chancellery in Bonn following a night of pub crawling. "I want in!" he supposedly bellowed, shaking the main entrance gate. The ambitious parliamentarian finally got his wish the following decade, when he became the first member of the postwar generation to serve as chancellor. A trained attorney born in 1944, Schröder first joined the SPD in the early 1960s and, in 1978, became chair of the party's youth organization, the *Jusos* (Young Socialists), where he was associated with its more leftist wing. Two years later, the self-described "resolute Marxist" – who would later become a confidant of Vladimir Putin and work on behalf of Russian energy companies – entered the Bundestag.[1] In 1990, he became the minister president of Lower Saxony, a position he held until winning the chancellorship in the fall of 1998.

Already in the late 1970s, Schröder suggested that he was open to working together with the Greens, who, like him, chose to make a political statement by dressing informally in the Bundestag. So, it was not a complete surprise when, two decades later, he formed the first "Red–Green" coalition between the SPD and the upstart environmentalist peace party, which, following unification, had merged with a group of former East German dissidents to create Alliance 90/The Greens. Joschka Fischer, the rechristened party's leading figure, became deputy chancellor and foreign minister in 1998 – the first time a Green served in this capacity. Fifteen years earlier, when Fischer had entered the Bundestag as a member of the first Green parliamentary faction in 1983, few would have predicted his later ascendancy to such a lofty position. The future foreign minister had first become active politically in the late 1960s as a militant, street-fighting "urban guerrilla" in the leftist, "extra-parliamentary" scene. The German Autumn of 1977 was a turning point for Fischer, who now eschewed violence in favor of the more traditional political process. Five years later, he joined the Greens and quickly became associated with its more pragmatic wing, the so-called *Realos* (realists).

The Red–Green Coalition in an Era of Reform

Given the somewhat similar political pedigrees and trajectories of these two savvy public figures – from staunch, rough-and-tumble leftists to moderate leaders of two of Germany's major mainstream parties – the Red–Green coalition they formed in 1998 seemed, if not a match made in heaven, not entirely incongruous. Indeed, during their first term in office, which lasted until 2002, the new governing partners successfully introduced a raft of progressive reforms near and dear to the hearts of the parties' rank-and-file. These included a promise to phase out the use of nuclear power within thirty years, making the Federal Republic the first industrial nation to take on that commitment. The coalition pledged to focus instead on the development of renewable energies, and, to that end, introduced a new "ecotax" on electricity. (Green proposals to increase the tax on petrol to a whopping 5 DM per liter and introduce a speed limit on the famed German autobahn proved less popular and had to be withdrawn.)

The Red–Green reforms were not just limited to these and other environmentally friendly policies aimed at combatting climate change. A new law adopted in 2001 allowed for same-sex civil unions. Citizenship and naturalization laws were liberalized as well, making it possible for those born in Germany to foreign nationals to acquire citizenship by birthright. Up to that point, *jus sanguinis* ("right of blood") had long been the law of the land, limiting citizenship solely to descent – that is, to the children of at least one "ethnically" German parent. In another move intended to make the Federal Republic more hospitable to foreigners, a new "green card" program based on the American model temporarily made it easier to recruit IT specialists from outside Germany and the European Union. As this suggests, the challenges of remaining economically competitive slowly whittled away longstanding prejudices against the idea of Germany as a land of immigration, especially as the "native" German population aged.

The Federal Republic had not seen the adoption of so many domestic reforms since Willy Brandt's chancellorship in the early 1970s. This new era of reform was a concerted effort to "modernize" Germany in response to mounting challenges in an increasingly globalized world. Six months after (barely) winning the federal election of September 2002, Schröder's second government unveiled an audacious plan to stimulate the economy and reduce doggedly high unemployment levels of nearly 12 percent: "Agenda 2010," widely hailed – and condemned – as the greatest reform of the labor market in the history of the Federal Republic.

For one, it weakened existing laws to make it easier to hire and fire employees; it also allowed for more part-time and "temporary" work. There were other "neoliberal" elements as well, primarily intended to reduce state spending: sweeping cuts in outlays for social welfare benefits, as well as tax breaks for individuals and businesses. Workers and employees now had to pay higher social security contributions – at the same time the number of benefits covered by public health insurance plans and the length of time one could receive unemployment benefits were both reduced.

A series of measures known as "Hartz IV" (named for Peter Hartz, the head of the committee that had recommended the changes in the first place) combined welfare and jobless benefits for the long-term unemployed, who now received a monthly pittance from the state: less than 400 euros. Hartz IV combined carrots and sticks, reminiscent of similar welfare reforms introduced by moderate leftists elsewhere: Bill Clinton in the US and Tony Blair in the UK. The government increased education opportunities and support for retraining, but those who refused to accept a "legitimate" job offer suffered serious sanctions, including a reduction of monthly payments by the state. Penalties against the supposedly "work-shy" had time-honored traditions in Germany – long before and, especially in the GDR, *after* 1945.

After decades of extremely generous social benefits, German society finally had to pay the piper and endure painful reductions in state support. Perhaps only a leftist politician like Schröder could have introduced such cuts. But the backlash was swift, also from within the chancellor's own party. His rival Oskar Lafontaine, who had earlier resigned from his position as minister of finance over policy disputes, quit the SPD and helped create a new party, *Die Linke* (The Left), which subsequently absorbed the PDS and went on to enjoy considerable electoral success, especially in the former East, thanks to its left-wing populist political message.

Still, Schröder's leftist credentials made it somewhat easier for his government to push through unpopular social and economic reforms. In a similar way, those of Green foreign minister Joschka Fischer had made an equally controversial decision a bit more palatable, this time in the area of foreign policy. Four years after the end of the brutal war in Bosnia, new hostilities erupted in the Balkans. In response to Serb aggression toward the Albanian minority in Kosovo, NATO launched a series of air attacks against Serbia and Serb forces starting in March 1999 – without a UN mandate. This time Germans carried out bombing missions aboard Tornado fighter aircraft, marking a true caesura in the postwar history of the Federal Republic. This was the first combat deployment of German armed forces since 1945.

There was much debate at home about that decision, which Fischer justified by pointing once again to the weight of German history. Responding to reports of renewed ethnic cleansing and other Serb atrocities in Kosovo, the foreign minister argued that Germans could not stand aside while a possible genocide was taking place. Just as he had four years earlier in the wake of the Srebrenica massacre, Fischer once again invoked the charged dictum, "Never again Auschwitz!" He came out in full support of German military participation in a "humanitarian intervention," a euphemistic new catchphrase of the 1990s. Not all Greens were convinced. In the name of pacifism, an antiwar protester symbolically threw a bag of red paint at Fischer at a major party gathering that May, covering him in "blood" and perforating one of his eardrums.

Adopting less violent methods, many in Germany and elsewhere questioned the legality of the NATO mission, especially in the absence of a UN mandate. Other critics charged that German participation represented a break with a major tenet of (West) Germany's postwar foreign policy, namely, a staunch commitment to multilateralism. But multilateralism had always meant working together with the Federal Republic's Western allies, and, in that sense, participation in the Kosovo War was no departure from precedent; in fact, it only reconfirmed that commitment.

Terrorism and *Leitkultur*

That would change just a few years later, following the terrorist attacks of September 11, 2001. At first, Schröder declared his country's full support for and "unconditional solidarity" with the United States. That November, the Bundestag voted in favor of a government motion to send troops to Afghanistan to help defeat the Taliban and Al-Qaeda. German security would "also be defended at the Hindu Kush," Minister of Defense Peter Struck confidently declared. The Federal Republic wound up sending the second largest contingent to Afghanistan, approximately 150,000 troops over a twenty-year period.[2]

But less than a year and a half later, the German chancellor balked at American president George W. Bush's request that the Federal Republic join the so-called Coalition of the Willing, an international military effort to overthrow Iraqi dictator Saddam Hussein. Germany would not participate in any unnecessary military "adventures," Schröder explained, especially ones that were not clearly in the country's own national interests.[3] Domestic political considerations also played a role. The chancellor was in the middle of a federal election campaign, and the looming war in Iraq was extremely unpopular in Germany.

Whatever his reasons, Schröder's stubborn refusal reflected, even embodied, Germany's heightened degree of self-confidence on the world stage following unification. It also marked a postwar nadir in German–American relations. What it did not mean, however, was that the Federal Republic was blind to *genuine* dangers of terrorism, global or homegrown. After all, the country had previously amassed a great deal of experience on that score, already passing a series of anti-terror laws in the mid- and late 1970s in response to domestic terror attacks by the RAF. Even earlier, following the terrorist attack in Munich in 1972, authorities had created the so-called GSG 9, a federal police unit responsible for combatting terrorism. In short, many of the civil and juridical instruments necessary for combatting terrorism were already in place. But the horrific events of September 11, as well as a series of subsequent terror attacks in Europe itself – including one at a Christmas market in Berlin in December 2016, which left more than a dozen people dead – seemed to represent a new type of challenge that demanded a new type of response, just as the newfangled phenomenon of stagflation had demanded a novel economic response in the 1970s (see chapter 4).

The upshot was a series of more stringent laws and security measures intended to fight Political Islam and global terrorism, especially after it was revealed that several of the individuals responsible for carrying out the attacks of September 11 had lived and studied for several years in Hamburg, undetected and unchecked. A series of "anti-terror" security "packages" introduced a variety of measures intended to prevent further attacks, including the right to forbid religious organizations deemed dangerous. Possibilities for authorities to gain access to previously protected private information about "suspect" individuals also grew. Like elsewhere in Europe and the West, biometric information stored in microchips was now included on official documents like passports.

This triggered an indignant backlash in some quarters, with critics questioning the legality of the new laws, warning about their potential misuse, and worrying about the breakdown of the rule of law. These were especially fraught issues in Germany, which had lived through no less than *two* dictatorships over the past century. But just as officials had defended the inclusion a half century earlier of Article 6 in the Basic Law – which allowed for the prohibition of political parties deemed dangerously undemocratic – authorities argued that extreme measures limiting basic liberties were sometimes necessary to defend freedom and democracy.

There was also a different type of backlash at the time: mounting xenophobia, especially toward Muslims. This was nothing new, of course. Widespread Islamophobia had emerged long before September 11, partly in response to the Iranian revolution of 1979 and the rise of Political Islam. But as the twentieth century drew to a close, leading German academics and journalists initiated a public discussion about "assimilating" the growing number of immigrants whose traditions and values were ostensibly at odds with ones dominant in the Federal Republic. They floated the idea of a German "guiding culture" (*Leitkultur*), consisting of core, "universal" (read: Western) values, including respect for secularism, democracy, and human rights – not least for women.[4]

About a year before the destruction of the World Trade Center in New York City, prominent conservative politicians in the CDU/CSU publicly embraced – one might say, hijacked – this concept of a dominant or "guiding culture," largely for political and electoral purposes. The idea was that all who lived in Germany, regardless of their ethnic background, religion, or place of birth, were to adhere to a common set of social rules and guidelines – and, of course, speak and understand German. This came largely in response to growing talk on the Left about the allure of "multiculturalism," as well as to Red–Green efforts to introduce more generous citizenship and migration laws. But once the leftists lost power, discussion about the need for a *Leitkultur* quickly ran out of steam – at least for the time being.

Angela Merkel and the Debt Crisis

Federal elections in the fall of 2005 resulted in a narrow defeat for the governing coalition. There were a number of reasons for this, including a massive backlash against Agenda 2010, as well as a strong showing by The Left, the newly established party led by former SPD chancellor candidate-turned-renegade Oskar Lafontaine and former head of the PDS, Gregor Gysi. The close election results allowed for only one viable governing coalition, and in November 2005, the first of several Grand Coalitions was formed by the SPD and the CDU/CSU. After intense negotiations, former East German Angela Merkel – the first female leader of the CDU and the first female candidate for chancellor – became the first female leader of the Federal Republic *and* the first chancellor actually born in the Federal Republic.

Merkel, the daughter of a Protestant pastor, had moved with her family to the GDR while still an infant in the mid-1950s. She later earned a doctorate in quantum chemistry, working for several years as a research scientist, but decided to enter politics following the "peaceful revolution" of 1989. A protégée of Helmut Kohl, Merkel held several ministerial positions in the 1990s before becoming chancellor in late

2005 – one of only a handful of former East Germans to reach such an exalted political position in unified Germany.

Merkel would go on to serve as chancellor for just over sixteen years, making her tenure in office the third longest in German history – right behind the two chancellors of German unity, Otto von Bismarck and (by just days) her patron Helmut Kohl. She became known and respected for her calm if prim public demeanor, her intimate knowledge of the issues, as well as her knack for reaching consensus, even with political rivals. As the head of no less than three Grand Coalitions with the SPD (2005–9, 2013–17, and 2018–21), that last talent was especially valuable. Following the election of Donald Trump as president of the United States in 2016, the British and American media crowned her the "leader of the free world," attesting to her growing stature – as well as that of unified Germany.[5] Merkel nevertheless faced two major challenges during her chancellorship: a global (and later European) economic meltdown, and a major refugee crisis which translated into growing electoral support for the xenophobic extreme right.

The world financial catastrophe that began in 2008, just three years after Merkel became the new head of government, was not the first sign of the potential pitfalls of neoliberalism and deregulation, "globalization" (*the* buzzword of the 1990s), and a transformative era of new information technology and telecommunications. That decade, normally risk-averse investors and "ordinary" Germans became caught up in a stock market frenzy triggered by the (partial) privatization of major public companies, including the state-run postal service.

A fervid rush to buy stock – first in Deutsche Telekom, a telecommunications behemoth set up in 1995, later in the plethora of new "dot-com" internet start-up companies – produced a bubble that, like all financial bubbles, eventually burst. Isolated voices warned at the time about the perils of unbridled neo-liberalism, including Oskar Lafontaine, who called for greater regulation of the financial markets. His prescient admonitions were largely ignored, just as they had been a half decade earlier during the rush to German unity.

Had his warnings not been written off as the mis-guided ravings of an extreme leftist, Germany and the world might have been spared, at least in part, the worst economic crisis since the Great Depression. Reckless speculation, especially in the real estate sector, almost led to the collapse of international banking and the global economy as a whole. But the so-called Great Recession, which began in 2008, was just the start of a decade of economic chaos and mass unemployment. A fresh crisis emerged a year later, this time in the heart of the new European Union, which had just adopted a common currency a decade earlier. In the lead-up to the introduction of the euro in 1999, European leaders established a set of eco-nomic criteria for those states wishing to join. This included a pledge to limit a given country's state debt to no more than 60 percent of its GDP.

The Federal Republic had difficulty meeting that goal, but the worst offender by far was Greece, which falsified the financial information it supplied to the EU. This resulted in a massive debt crisis and major recession that brought Greece to the brink of defaulting on its international loans. That posed a major danger for foreign banks, especially German ones. Hoping to avoid another major economic crisis so soon after the start of the Great Recession, the EU agreed to a series of bailouts, with wealthy Germany underwriting a sizable portion of those loans. In return, the Germans and Greece's other foreign creditors insisted that the Mediterranean country adopt a series of austerity measures and structural reforms intended to restore its economic well-being.

By demanding massive sacrifices, those stringent conditions created a great deal of hardship, suffering, and bad blood in Greece – just as the loans themselves were highly unpopular in Germany, where many thought that their "profligate" neighbors to the south should pull their own chestnuts out of the fire. The Greeks responded in kind, dredging up hoary national stereotypes and making fodder of Germany's dark past. Their media portrayed leading German officials, including Merkel, in Nazi uniforms and Hitler-like mustaches. Horst Reichenbach, the head of an EU task force sent to Greece in late 2011, was wittily, if tastelessly, referred to as "Third Reichenbach."[6]

The British media would later take similar potshots at the "krauts" in the run-up to Brexit, the UK's withdrawal from the EU following a national referendum in 2016.

But criticism of the Germans went beyond cheap and nasty historical digs. Foreign observers, in Greece and elsewhere, accused Berlin of sheer hypocrisy. They pointed, for instance, to Germany's own difficulties fulfilling the criteria for joining the Eurozone. At the same time, they blamed "greedy" German banks for "enabling" Greece's irresponsible financial behavior in the first place. Critics pointed above all to the Federal Republic's massive foreign trade surplus. This, they claimed, had significantly contributed to the dire economic straits of Greece and Germany's other less well-off neighbors, who had taken out loans to purchase exports that were "Made in Germany." In a sense, the same dynamic that had got the economies of Eastern Europe into hot water in the 1980s and eventually led to the downfall of those regimes – namely, excessive foreign debt – was now plaguing the Federal Republic's partners in the EU.

By the time the state-debt crisis exploded, their very number was increasing apace, from twelve member states the year the Berlin Wall fell to twenty-eight in 2013. (That number decreased by one after Brexit became official in 2020.) The Federal Republic was strongly in favor of EU expansion to Eastern Europe for political and economic reasons, as well as out of a sense of historical responsibility. It hoped to ensure stability in a region where (like Greece, incidentally) the Wehrmacht had rampaged in the 1940s – *and* that offered a promising market for German exports. Like Willy Brandt's Ostpolitik in the early 1970s, and in the wake of Hans-Dietrich Genscher's pressure to recognize the independence of Croatia and Slovenia in the early 1990s, German interests and actions in the region worried the country's skittish partners in the West, who, suspecting more selfish motives, proved impervious to German pretentions to be acting selflessly "in Europe's name."[7]

The Refugee Crisis and the Rise of the Extreme Right

A massive refugee crisis that began in the 2010s – a product of civil war and other violence in places like Syria and Afghanistan, Libya and Sudan – further fanned the flames of anti-German sentiment. After some initial hesitation, Angela Merkel announced in late August 2015 that the Federal Republic would be suspending an EU regulation that allowed member states to refuse asylum to persons who had previously been in a "safe" third country outside their own. This 2013 agreement hewed closely to a similar reform adopted by Germany two decades earlier during the war in Bosnia. In July 1993, in an attempt to stanch the inflow of refugees from the Balkans and elsewhere, the government had introduced a massive overhaul of the rules governing asylum, effectively cutting off all land access to the Federal Republic – at least in theory. Smugglers had different ideas on this score.

Now moved by the images of death and destruction, especially in Syria, the chancellor essentially opened the door to foreigners in need who had already made it to Southern Europe. The number of asylum applications increased more than fivefold in a year, and more than a million refugees subsequently arrived. "We'll manage this!" Merkel optimistically assured her fellow citizens – many of whom were still waiting impatiently for Kohl's "blooming landscapes" to materialize in the East.[8]

Germany's European partners, especially the EU's newest member states in Eastern Europe, were appalled by Merkel's rogue decision. For one, they were angered that she had not consulted them beforehand; more important, they balked at distribution quotas that would ease Germany's burden by spreading the refugees – and the responsibility for their care and upkeep – across Europe. Just as it had during the Balkans wars of the 1990s, a mixture of moral considerations and the enduring weight of the Nazi past accounted for Merkel's undeniable largesse. And, at first, many ordinary Germans supported her démarche. Praised for their country's new *Willkommenskultur* (welcoming culture), millions provided various forms of support and humanitarian assistance to these poor souls fleeing war-torn regions. But then the backlash began.

In early 2013, a group of disgruntled conservatives, including economists and former members of the CDU, established the Alternative for Germany (*Alternative für Deutschland*, AfD), a new political party whose main message initially focused on opposition to the Eurozone's economic policies – including, not least, the recent Greek bailout. It quickly moved to the extreme right in the wake of the refugee crisis, espousing a blatantly xenophobic agenda. Another far-right movement also formed at this time, Patriotic Europeans Against the Islamization of the West (PEGIDA), which, from the outset, spread an openly anti-Muslim, anti-establishment, and anti-globalization message. In a grotesque throwback to the "Monday demonstrations" that had taken place in Leipzig in the fall of 1989, the founders of PEGIDA organized a series of mass demonstrations in the nearby eastern German city of Dresden, beginning in the fall of 2014. The number of participants peaked at roughly 25,000 in January 2015.[9]

The rise of PEGIDA and the AfD marked a decisive sea change in political discourse, which, as in the United States under Donald Trump, became decidedly racist and unabashedly nationalistic, coarser, and more aggressive – especially in the anonymous online world of the internet and social media. Fueled by a growing sense of economic insecurity in an increasingly globalized world, these two populist, xenophobic, anti-refugee movements gave voice to angry disappointment with and alienation from the mainstream political and cultural establishment.

This was not limited to the Federal Republic. The 2016 Brexit campaign in the United Kingdom and the 2017 Yellow Vests protests in France were both cut, more or less, from the same cloth. Xenophobia, racism, and violence against foreigners were nothing new, but they became more politically and socially acceptable as the number of refugees from Muslim-majority countries seeking safe haven in Europe surged. Support for the extreme right was not limited to the former East, but it was especially pronounced there, where, starting in 2017, the AfD made an impressive showing in local, state, and even federal elections. This had much to do with continuing disappointment about the aftermath of unification. The role played by the after-effects of having been socialized in the GDR, where most East Germans had had little contact with foreigners, is anyone's guess.

Merkel's CDU and the opposition Social Democrats booked their worst performances since 1949 but still managed to cobble together a governing coalition in 2017. The economically liberal FDP re-entered the parliament that year, after failing to satisfy the 5-percent electoral hurdle in 2013 – *another* first since the founding of the republic and, perhaps, punishment for the global economic crisis. The AfD now became the third largest party in parliament, the first time since the early 1950s that the extreme right was represented in the Bundestag. This was the price

Merkel paid for her unpopular stance on immigration. Elevated poverty levels played a role, too, with millions of Germans still stuck on the rolls of Hartz IV the year the election took place.

Economic insecurity, the scapegoating of foreigners, outrageous and far-fetched conspiracy theories, frustration with the slow-working machinery of parliamentary democracy, a growing sense of alienation from the political establishment, mainstream media, and other "elites": Was this the 1930s redux? In one sense, no. Starting around 2010, the Federal Republic enjoyed a sustained economic upswing, with positive growth rates and a reduction of unemployment levels by half. The painful reforms introduced by the Red–Green coalition certainly played a role here, as did soaring exports following the introduction of the euro. That alone differentiates this period from the earlier one. But it also makes the elevated levels of anger, resentment, and pessimism even more perplexing.

There were other alarming signs. In the 1990s, a neo-Nazi terrorist organization, the National Socialist Underground (NSU), was formed in the eastern German state of Thuringia. Between 2000 and 2007, its members killed a policewoman and nine immigrants, mainly of Turkish descent. They also carried out a series of bomb attacks and bank robberies, as well as dozens of other attempted murders of individuals with a "migration background." Undercover agents managed to infiltrate the organization, and in 2013, its ringleaders were put on trial in the largest judicial proceeding ever held in the Federal Republic against neo-Nazis. Their prison sentences ranged from several years to life imprisonment.

Disturbing parallels, to be sure. But the Federal Republic's democratic traditions and commitment to the rule of law have successfully protected the country from domestic threats thus far – in contradistinction to the Weimar Republic, where conservative justices frequently let off violent members of the extreme right with no more than a slap on the wrist. After leading the failed Beer Hall Putsch of November 1923, for example, Adolf Hitler received a five-year sentence that was later commuted to a mere eight months – enough time, still, for him to dictate *Mein Kampf*.

An Erratic Foreign Policy Era?

Unified Germany's greater self-confidence in the international arena and its increased willingness to deploy the Bundeswehr abroad set off alarm bells as well, among progressives at home and some foreign observers. But what really concerned the country's allies was its seemingly erratic foreign policy choices, especially its recurrent reluctance to participate in international military missions. Most concerning, abroad but also for many at home, was a controversial decision in March 2011 to abstain from a UN Security Council vote to impose a "no-fly zone" over Libya. A brutal civil war had just erupted there during the so-called Arab Spring, a series of anti-government protests and armed rebellions in the region that lasted for two years, beginning in late 2010. After abstaining from the vote, the Germans also refused to participate in UN-sanctioned military efforts to protect innocent civilians. This was a far cry from Kosovo a decade earlier, but very much in tune with Germany's decision not to take an active military role in the second Gulf War that began in March 2003.

Once again, the decision was motivated in no small part by *domestic* political considerations. State elections were scheduled for the week following the vote at the UN, and opinion surveys suggested just how unenthusiastic the overwhelming majority of ordinary citizens – already critical of German deployment in Afghanistan – felt about further military "adventures" abroad. Other considerations, including strategic and geopolitical ones, also played a role in the decision. But whatever the reasons cited by the chancellor and her foreign minister, Guido Westerwelle of the FDP, Berlin managed to alienate *all* its major allies in Europe and across the Atlantic.

But then, in a dramatic turnaround three years after its UN abstention, the country took a leading role in the response to the 2014 Russian invasion and annexation of Crimea. It helped usher through a raft of international economic and political sanctions, led by a new foreign minister, Frank-Walter Steinmeier of the SPD, who later became the twelfth president of the Federal Republic. The German government stepped up to the plate once again in early 2022, following

Moscow's full-scale invasion of Ukraine. Three days after Russian bombs began falling, Social Democrat Olaf Scholz, Merkel's successor since December, dropped a proverbial bomb of his own.

At a special session of the Bundestag on February 27, the new chancellor announced that the world was experiencing a "*Zeitenwende*" – a watershed moment, a historical turning point, an epochal shift – and that this called for a decisive response. That was why, he continued, the government planned to set up a "special fund" involving a one-time investment of 100 billion euros to make the Bundeswehr "ultramodern" and provide it with "bold, new capabilities." Germany would also fulfill one of NATO's longstanding goals by annually investing at least 2 percent of its GDP in defense. That was "a great deal of money," Scholz conceded, but it was important to protect "our freedom and democracy."[10]

Environmental Challenges amid Growing Political Polarization

Gerhard Schröder, Angela Merkel, and Olaf Scholz all faced a number of serious challenges during their tenure in office: a global economic meltdown, a major refugee crisis, the political rise of the extreme right, Russian aggression in Eastern Europe, and, last but not least, the COVID pandemic, which, by giving rise to many conspiracy theories, increased support for fringe parties on the left and right.

There was yet another emergency that assumed catastrophic proportions under their chancellorships, one that posed an existential threat to all of humanity – namely, the effects of climate change. In the summer of 2002, the Federal Republic experienced the worst natural disaster in its history, when heavy rains flooded the Elbe River, killing dozens, leading to mass evacuations, and leaving thousands homeless in the East. In 2018, Germans experienced a different form of extreme weather: the hottest year on record (at the time) since the late nineteenth century, resulting in a sustained drought that emptied most of Germany's main rivers, including the Rhine.

The rise of the Green Party in the late 1970s had first turned the attention of large numbers of Germans, primarily in the West but also in the East, to the dangerous consequences of environmental degradation. The Federal Republic would subsequently take a leading global role in the environmental movement, serving as a model for other industrial countries – much as it served as a model for dealing with difficult memories of a dark historical past. The Germans signed on to and vigorously supported major international agreements intended to reduce carbon dioxide emissions and other environmental contaminants. They also introduced innovative recycling programs while becoming a world leader in the renewable energy sector. The Federal Republic even pledged to phase out the use of nuclear and coal power plants and satisfy the majority of its energy needs with "biomass," wind, and solar power before the year 2040. These are all admirable goals, but the country still has a long way to go. It remains one of the world's largest producers of greenhouse gases and consistently fails to meet self-imposed environmental deadlines.

Still, by the start of the twenty-first century, all the major political parties in Germany had jumped on the "Green bandwagon," incorporating pro-environmental policies into their platforms – or at least paying lip service to such concerns. Following the Fukushima nuclear accident in Japan in 2011, the CDU and FDP abandoned their staunch opposition to the Red–Green coalition's controversial decision in 2002 to halt all reliance on nuclear energy by the early 2020s. The "greening" of the political landscape was only one way in which the Federal Republic's traditional "political colors" started to bleed into one another. As some pundits – and critics – have observed, a "black" (read: conservative) pall hung over Schröder's neoliberal reforms. A decade later, the policies of the CDU seemed distinctly "redder" (progressive) than ever before. One thinks of Merkel's generous refugee policies, which cost her so much political goodwill, prompting estranged party members and voters to gravitate toward the extreme right.

This "social democratization" of the CDU and "Christian democratization" of the SPD helped make possible the three Grand Coalitions that formed between 2005 and 2021. Essential differences remained between the two parties, to be sure. But the growing perception that they were becoming more and more alike – *and* that they were unable to address, much less solve, issues of great concern to German voters – led to their waning electoral success and, in turn, greater support for newer, upstart parties like the AfD. This made working coalitions between the Federal Republic's two oldest "catch-all people's parties" more and more difficult to achieve – one reason why federal elections in 2021 resulted in a so-called traffic-light coalition between the "red" SPD, the "yellow" FDP, and the Greens. Olaf Scholz's government had a difficult time reaching consensus on a number of major issues, from budget outlays to new regulations for heating private homes. This constant infighting was a major reason for its unpopularity, and it finally led to the collapse of the fragile coalition in November 2024.

This followed on the heels of a string of astounding electoral successes by the AfD earlier that year, when it came in second (after the CDU/CSU) in European Parliamentary elections *and* became the first far-right party in Germany since the National Socialists to win a plurality of seats in a state election – in Thuringia, no less, where a Nazi had joined a state government for the first time in 1929. Growing polarization on the political edges and the difficulty of forging working coalitions were a major reason why Germany's first democracy fell apart, culminating in Hitler's appointment as chancellor in 1933. At a time when even countries with more venerable democratic conditions, like the United States, seem to be on the verge of succumbing to more autocratic styles of government, it remains to be seen whether the Federal Republic will experience a similar fate. If it does, the German Question will surely return with a vengeance.

Epilogue

On November 10, 1989, prominent West German politicians gathered in front of West Berlin's city hall to celebrate the momentous event that had taken place the day before: the breaching of the Berlin Wall. They addressed the large crowd that had come together on precisely the same spot John F. Kennedy had delivered his famous "Ich bin ein Berliner" speech a quarter century earlier. A different "one-liner" would now become associated with that storied venue, uttered this time by the very same person who had hosted the American president so many years before. According to legend, former chancellor Willy Brandt told the crowd that evening, "What belongs together will now grow together." He did not actually use those precise words, but the soundbite – and sentiment – stuck. Germany *and* Europe would now finally overcome forty years of division.

Something else took place that evening that was also memorable, but for different reasons. At the end of his own remarks, Helmut Kohl, accompanied by the other dignitaries at his side, began to sing the German national hymn. Instead of joining in, the crowd laughed and booed mercilessly, as they had throughout the chancellor's entire speech. The leftist newspaper *Die*

Tageszeitung inserted in its next edition a cheap vinyl recording that captured the embarrassing moment for posterity. The souvenir issue quickly sold out.

Those who booed that evening were making a political statement about the chancellor, who, for his part, later dismissed them as "leftist trash."[1] But their cheeky response to the national hymn also revealed something about nationalist sentiment in the West – or, rather, about its absence. For all the ecstatic joy that greeted the fall of the Wall, national unity was far from most minds at that moment.[2] For decades, West Germans – especially those born after the war or without friends or family "over there" – had become less and less interested in the fate of the GDR, less and less connected to and concerned about those "stuck" in the East. Their leaders continued to pay lip service to unification, but the idea of a united German nation became increasingly unfamiliar, almost abstract.

That would soon change, thanks in no small part to those East Germans who took to the streets in the fall of 1989. But a desire for unity was by no means self-evident at the time, on either side of the Wall. Leading GDR dissidents showed little initial interest in some sort of unification. Many "ordinary" East Germans, for their part, continued to harbor feelings of resentment toward the Federal Republic, where, for decades, West European unity seemed more urgent and more important than *German* unity. By turning their gaze westward and embracing "Europe" as an ersatz for the nation after the horrors of the Third Reich, their brethren in the West had seemingly turned their backs on the East and effectively written off those who lived there. This was especially galling, given that they were not the ones who had suffered most and longest from the consequences of World War II. Those feelings of resentment quickly subsided, though they would later resurface during the painful process of unification and "transformation" in the East.

In any event, long dormant national feelings *did* emerge over the next twelve months – for those in the GDR, a cynic might argue, thanks to the allure of the deutschmark (not to mention the victory of the German soccer team in the World Cup that summer). Material considerations certainly played a role in the East, as did the desire for democracy, greater civil liberties, and the right to travel. But there were other reasons why feelings of national cohesiveness appeared to resurface seemingly overnight, despite four decades of division. Years of doffing one's cap to unity had kept the idea alive in the Federal Republic, a place that, in turn, never became entirely "foreign" to most East Germans – thanks to years of listening in secret to Western media, as well as greater interpersonal contact with Westerners following Ostpolitik. A common language, culture, and historical memory also sustained national feelings on both sides of the Elbe. The SED regime had done its part here, "rediscovering" and publicly revalorizing Prusso-German historical traditions and "virtues" in the 1980s.

Hitler's noxious policies may have brutally discredited German nationalism, but they could not entirely undo Bismarck's successful nation-building efforts of the late nineteenth century.

Persistent differences and lingering resentments between so-called Ossis and Wessis have nevertheless made internal unification a difficult and ongoing process. Ironically, overcoming political division turned out to be far easier, in the end, than surmounting the human divisions produced by forty years of separation. Still, if stability and longevity are any measure, unification has largely been a success. The "new" Federal Republic has now lasted longer than Weimar and the Third Reich combined, and the two German states – and peoples – have indeed "grown together," as Willy Brandt predicted more than thirty-five years ago. The themes explored in this book illuminate and help explain the trials, tribulations, *and* achievements of that process. But does it mean the German Question has finally been put to rest?

***

The wintry month of November 2024 began with two major political "surprises." Donald Trump won re-election on November 5. The very next day, German chancellor Olaf Scholz dismissed finance minister Christian Lindner of the FDP, citing irreconcilable differences. The increasingly dysfunctional "traffic-light" coalition had taken its last gasp (see p. 206), and snap elections were called for late February.

In the run-up to the German election, the new American president upended decades of US foreign policy after taking office on January 20, 2025, cozying up to Russian dictator Vladimir Putin and essentially making it clear that Europe could no longer count on American security guarantees. The future of NATO seemed to be in serious doubt. In mid-February, Trump's vice president, J.D. Vance, informed European leaders at the annual Munich Security Conference that the greatest "threat" confronting their continent was not an "external" one posed by Russia or China, but rather one "from within, the retreat of Europe from some of its most fundamental values." He was referring to efforts aimed at countering the rise of far-right, anti-immigrant political parties, including the Federal Republic's Alternative for Germany (AfD). Few must have missed the chilling irony of an American politician lecturing his listeners – gathered together in a country where, almost a century earlier, almost half of the electorate had voted for the Nazis in the last (relatively) free election prior to their "seizure of power" – that "democracy rests on the sacred principle that the voice of the people matters."[3]

A month earlier, during an interview livestreamed on X (formerly Twitter), tech billionaire Elon Musk – who would soon play an influential role in the Trump administration – had heaped effusive praise upon and effectively endorsed AfD chief Alice Weidel, the upstart party's candidate for chancellor in the upcoming election. Such blatant interference in a close ally's electoral process was alarming and remarkable, if not entirely unprecedented. But it was no surprise: the new American administration and the European far-right hold similar views on the need to close national borders, halt immigration, and deport ("remigrate") certain groups of "undesirable" foreigners en masse. Such positions have led to widespread accusations that the AfD is an extremist party that poses a threat to democracy in Germany. The use of Nazi slogans and rhetoric by several of its leaders has only bolstered that impression – even if calls to *close* borders are not quite the same, yet, as efforts to *expand* them.

Given the xenophobic party's surge in polling over the previous year, it was small wonder that all eyes were focused on the outcome of the February 23 federal election and any signs of German "backsliding" – *despite* promises by the mainstream parties not to form a coalition government with the AfD regardless of its electoral showing, a policy known as the "firewall." The results were not cataclysmic, but they were also not entirely reassuring. The conservative CDU/CSU came in first, and the members of the old coalition – the SPD, the Greens, and the FDP – all bled votes. The AfD placed second with almost 21 percent, doubling its support since the last federal election in 2021. A recent series of dramatic terror attacks, carried out by Muslim migrants from Syria and Saudi Arabia, contributed in no small measure to the outcome of an election dominated by concerns about immigration and the economy. But the so-called firewall held, and the AfD was left out in the cold, despite its impressive showing. On May 6, the new chancellor, Friedrich Merz of the CDU/CSU, officially formed a new coalition government with the SPD.[4]

The outcome of the election was nevertheless disconcerting. In contrast to its performance in the West, the AfD received the highest proportion of votes in almost every constituency located in the former GDR, underscoring just how divided the country remained along East/West lines. Equally notable was the influence that voter age had on the election results. According to exit polls, more than half of all young people between ages eighteen and twenty-four cast their ballots for populist parties on the extremes of the political spectrum: the AfD and The Left, as well as an offshoot of the latter, the so-called Sahra Wagenknecht Alliance. From the perspective of the mainstream parties and electorate, that did not bode well for the future. Nor did racist rhetoric and anti-immigrant violence in a country suffering from a stagnating economy. This set off all sorts of alarm bells. Might Germany one day pose a danger once again to itself and its neighbors? In other words, was the dreaded German Question on the verge of making a come-back?

Hardly. Or at least not in the way one might expect, as Robert Kagan argued in "The New German Question," an essay that appeared in the spring of 2019 in the journal *Foreign Affairs*. The neoconservative scholar identified possible shifts in the global environment that could lead to the demise of the "democratic and peace-loving Germany everyone knows and loves." What might happen, Kagan asked, if the main pillars of the post-1945 world order were to tumble, including those initially designed to keep Germany in check and "moored to the liberal world"? If, in other words, American security guarantees and the international free-trade regime were to erode – at a time when anti-European nationalism was making inroads on the continent and authoritarian forms of leadership were enjoying a come-back – how long would it be before "new generations of Germans" began to adopt "normal geopolitical ambitions, normal selfish interests, and normal nationalist pride"?[5] He didn't define "normal," but he didn't really need to: the ominous message was clear.

A staunch critic of Donald Trump, Kagan wrote these words in the middle of the first MAGA presidency. The second Trump administration has since taken off the gloves, imposing steep tariffs on foreign imports (despite the dire lessons of destabilizing economic nationalism during the interwar period), placating Vladimir Putin and other foreign dictators, even telling reporters a year earlier that the Russians could "do whatever the hell they want" if the Europeans refused to pay more for their own defense.[6]

Trump's threats and policies mean that Germany, a country heavily dependent on foreign exports and the American nuclear umbrella, is at a crossroads. So, too, are its partners in the EU. But if the postwar European project fails and the German Question were to return with a vengeance, it would not be Trump's fault alone. Old nationalist and economic antagonisms had already begun to resurface before his surprise election in 2016: during the Eurozone crisis and Brexit campaign, and in the wake of mass migration from the developing world. Virulent xenophobia and staunch criticism of "Europe" – including the supranational institutions that had successfully kept Germany tame and old nationalist rivalries at bay for decades – have been major sources of the far-right's popularity, in Germany and elsewhere.

It could turn out, of course, that the Trump presidency has just the opposite effect, with an international trade war and the sudden absence of an American security guarantee bringing Europeans *closer* together. As conservative CDU leader Friedrich Merz commented right after his party's victory on February 23, "My absolute priority will be to strengthen Europe as quickly as possible so that, step by step, we can really achieve independence from the USA . . . I never thought I would have to say something like this . . . But after Donald Trump's statements last week . . . it is clear that the Americans . . . are largely indifferent to the fate of Europe."[7] That was astounding, coming from an avowed trans-Atlanticist.

Up to now, reliance on American military protection has allowed Germany (and Europe) to funnel vast sums of money into generous social welfare programs instead of a costly arms build-up. This has been an important source of domestic stability since World War II. Putin's invasion of Ukraine and Trump's "America-first" policies have changed the calculus, however, and the Germans will now need to rethink their funding priorities, a potential source of political *instability* at home. If recent developments continue along the same trajectory, the German Question might indeed make a come-back one day – this time in response to the "New *American* Question."

Ann Arbor, February 25, 2025

Further Reading

Some of the finest work on modern German history has appeared in English or in translation, which is fortunate for readers who do not read German but are eager to learn more about the topics covered in this book. For a quick overview of the grand sweep of German history, see M. Fulbrook, *A Concise History of Germany*, 3rd ed. (Cambridge University Press, 2019); also see the essays in H.W. Smith, ed., *The Oxford Handbook of Modern German History* (Oxford University Press, 2011).

Useful surveys of the twentieth and twenty-first centuries include U. Herbert, *A History of Twentieth-Century Germany* (Oxford University Press, 2019); M. Fulbrook, *A History of Germany, 1918–2020: The Divided Nation*, 5th ed. (Wiley Blackwell, 2021); H.A. Turner, Jr., *Germany from Partition to Reunification*, rev. ed. (Yale University Press, 1992); M. Gehler, *Three Germanies: From Partition to Unification and Beyond*, 2nd ed. (Reaktion, 2021). Also see M. Fulbrook, *The People's State: East German Society from Hitler to Honecker* (Yale University Press, 2005); J. Sneeringer, *West Germany: A Society in Motion, 1949–89* (Bloomsbury, 2024).

For thoughtful discussions about the "reinvention" of Germans after 1945, see F. Trentmann, *Out of the Darkness: The Germans, 1942–2022* (Knopf, 2024); K. Jarausch, *After Hitler: Recivilizing Germans, 1945–1995* (Oxford University Press, 2006). For innovative approaches to the post-1945 period, see the essays in C. Kleßmann, ed., *The Divided Past: Rewriting Post-War German History* (Berg, 2002); F. Bösch, ed., *A History Shared and Divided: East and West Germany since the 1970s* (Berghahn Books, 2018); A. Eckert and F. Biess, eds., "New Narratives for the History of the Federal Republic," *Central European History* 52, no. 1 (special issue, 2019). Also see F. Biess, *German Angst: Fear and Democracy in the Federal Republic of Germany* (Oxford University Press, 2020).

Lively accounts of the immediate postwar period include R. Bessel, *Germany 1945: From War to Peace* (Harper, 2009); H. Jähner, *Aftermath: Life in the Fallout of the Third Reich, 1945–1955* (Knopf, 2022); R.M. Douglas, *Orderly and Humane: The Expulsion of the Germans after the Second World War* (Yale University Press, 2012); F. Taylor, *Exorcising Hitler: The Occupation and Denazification of Germany* (Bloomsbury, 2011). Two important memoirs from this period are Anonymous, *A Woman in Berlin* (Virago, 2005); W. Leonhard, *Child of the Revolution* (Henry Regnery, 1958).

On specific Allied occupation policies, see N. Naimark, *The Russians in Germany: A History of the Soviet Zone of Occupation, 1945–1949* (The Belknap Press of Harvard University Press, 1995); R. Boehling, *A Question of Priorities: Democratic Reform and Economic Recovery in Postwar Germany* (Berghahn Books, 1996); R. Merritt, *Democracy Imposed: U.S. Occupation Policy and the German Public, 1945–1949* (Yale University Press, 1995); J. Tent, *Mission on the Rhine: "Reeducation" and Denazification in American-Occupied Germany* (University of Chicago Press, 1983); D. Phillips, *Educating the Germans: People and Policy in the British Zone of Germany, 1945–1949* (Bloomsbury, 2018); F.R. Willis, *The French in Germany, 1945–1949* (Stanford University Press, 1962).

"Denazification" and the Nuremberg trials are extensively covered in N. Frei, *Adenauer's Germany and the Nazi Past: The Politics of Amnesty and Integration* (Columbia University Press, 2002); M. Dack, *Everyday Denazification in Postwar Germany: The* Fragebogen *and Political Screening during the Allied Occupation* (Cambridge University Press, 2023); M. Marrus, *The Nuremberg War Crimes Trial, 1945–1946: A Documentary History* (Palgrave Macmillan, 1997). The "Nuremberg Trials Project" (https://nuremberg.law.harvard.edu/) is an online trove of primary sources.

On the "German Question," see D. Verheyen, *The German Question: A Cultural, Historical, and Geopolitical Exploration* (Routledge, 2019); W. Loth, *Stalin's Unwanted Child: The Soviet Union, the German Question and the Founding of the GDR* (Palgrave Macmillan, 1998); W. Gruner, "Is the German Question – Is the German Problem Back? The Role of Germany in Europe from an Historical Perspective," *Rivista di Studi Politici Internazionali* 84, no. 3 (2017): 341–73; M. Cresswell and M. Trachtenberg,

"France and the German Question, 1945–1955," *Journal of Cold War Studies* 5, no. 3 (2003): 5–28.

For foreign policy issues more generally, see H. Haftendorn, *Coming of Age: German Foreign Policy since 1945* (Rowman & Littlefield, 2006); R. Granieri, *The Ambivalent Alliance: Konrad Adenauer, the CDU/CSU, and the West, 1949–1966* (Berghahn Books, 2003); T. Schwarz, *America's Germany: John J. McCloy and the Federal Republic of Germany* (Harvard University Press, 1991); H. Harrison, *Driving the Soviets up the Wall: Soviet–East German Relations, 1953–1961* (Princeton University Press, 2003). On détente and Ostpolitik, see C. Fink and B. Schaefer, eds., *Ostpolitik, 1969–1974: European and Global Responses* (Cambridge University Press, 2008); W. Gray, *Germany's Cold War: The Global Campaign to Isolate East Germany, 1949–1969* (University of North Carolina Press, 2003); T.G. Ash, *In Europe's Name: Germany and the Divided Continent* (Knopf, 1993).

For an introduction to political structures and general political developments after 1945, see D. Patton, *Cold War Politics in Postwar Germany* (St. Martin's Press, 1999); P. Pulzer, *German Politics, 1945–1995* (Oxford University Press, 1996); P. Katzenstein, *Policy and Politics in West Germany* (Temple University Press, 1987). On constitutional issues and the Basic Law, see D. Kommers and R. Miller, *The Constitutional Jurisprudence of the Federal Republic of Germany*, 3rd ed. (Duke University Press, 2012).

On major politicians and political parties, see H.-P. Schwarz, *Konrad Adenauer*, 2 vols. (Berghahn Books, 1995 and 1997); M. Mitchell, *The Origins of Christian Democracy: Politics and Confession in Modern Germany* (University of Michigan Press, 2012); H. Miard-Delacroix, *Willy Brandt: Life of a Statesman* (I.B. Tauris, 2016); K. Spohr, *The Global Chancellor: Helmut Schmidt and the Reshaping of the International Order* (Oxford University Press, 2016); C. Wicke, *Helmut Kohl's Quest for Normality: His Representation of the German Nation and Himself* (Berghahn Books, 2015); "In Memory of the 'Two Helmuts': The Lives, Legacies, and Historical Impact of Helmut Schmidt and Helmut Kohl: A Forum," *Central European History* 51, no. 2 (2018): 282–309; J. Mushaben, *Becoming Madam Chancellor: Angela Merkel and the Berlin Republic* (Cambridge University Press, 2017); P. Hockenos,

Joschka Fischer and the Making of the Berlin Republic: An Alternative History of Postwar Germany (Oxford University Press, 2007); A. Markovits and P. Gorski, *The German Left: Red, Green, and Beyond* (Oxford University Press, 1993); D. Patton, *Out of the East: From PDS to Left Party in Unified Germany* (State University of New York Press, 2011).

On the economies of East and West Germany, see A.J. Nicholls, *Freedom with Responsibility: The Social Market Economy in Germany, 1918–1963* (Oxford University Press, 1994); A. Kramer, *The West German Economy, 1945–1955* (Bloomsbury, 1991); W. Gray, *Trading Power: West Germany's Rise to Global Influence, 1963–1975* (Oxford University Press, 2023); J. Kopstein, *The Politics of Economic Decline in East Germany, 1945–1989* (University of North Carolina Press, 1997); A. Steiner, *The Plans That Failed: An Economic History of the GDR* (Berghahn Books, 2010); J. Zatlin, *The Currency of Socialism: Money and Political Culture in East Germany* (Cambridge University Press, 2007); H. Berghoff and U. Balbier, eds., *Falling Behind or Catching Up? The East German Economy, 1945–2010* (Cambridge University Press, 2013).

For postwar consumption, culture, and social developments, see the essays in R. Moeller, ed., *West Germany under Construction: Politics, Society, and Culture in the Adenauer Era* (University of Michigan Press, 2007); H. Schissler, ed., *The Miracle Years: A Cultural History of West Germany, 1949–1968* (Princeton University Press, 2001); D. Crew, ed., *Consuming Germany in the Cold War* (Berg, 2003); M. Fulbrook and A.I. Port, eds., *Becoming East German: Socialist Structures and Sensibilities after Hitler* (Berghahn Books, 2013); K. Jarausch, ed., *Dictatorship as Experience: Towards a Socio-Cultural History of the GDR* (Berghahn Books, 1999); K. Pence and P. Betts, eds., *Socialist Modern: East German Everyday Culture and Politics* (University of Michigan Press, 2008).

More specialized studies include U. Poiger, *Jazz, Rock, and Rebels: Cold War Politics and American Culture in a Divided Germany* (University of California Press, 2000); M. Landsman, *Dictatorship and Demand: The Politics of Consumerism in East Germany* (Harvard University Press, 2005); M. Hoehn, *GIs and* Fräuleins*: The German-American Encounter in 1950s West Germany* (University of North Carolina Press, 2002); R. Pommerin, ed., *The American*

Impact on Postwar Germany (Berghahn Books, 1995); D. Pike, *The Politics of Culture in Soviet-Occupied Germany, 1945–1949* (Stanford University Press, 1992).

On environmental issues and the Greens, see F. Uekötter, *The Greenest Nation? A New History of German Environmentalism* (Oxford University Press, 2014); S. Milder, *Greening Democracy: The Anti-Nuclear Movement and Political Environmentalism in West Germany and Beyond, 1968–1983* (Cambridge University Press, 2017); A. Eckert, *West Germany and the Iron Curtain: Environment, Economy, and Culture in the Borderlands* (Oxford University Press, 2019); J. Ault, *Saving Nature Under Socialism: Transnational Environmentalism in East Germany, 1968–1990* (Cambridge University Press, 2021).

Few topics have aroused as much popular interest as repression in the GDR and the role of the Stasi. See J. Gieseke, *The History of the Stasi: East Germany's Secret Police, 1945–1990* (Berghahn Books, 2014); M. Dennis, *The Stasi: Myth and Reality* (Routledge, 2016); D. Childs, *The Stasi: The East German Intelligence and Security Service* (NYU Press, 1996); G. Bruce, *The Firm: The Inside Story of the Stasi* (Oxford University Press, 2010); P. Ahonen, *Death at the Berlin Wall* (Oxford University Press, 2011).

On "ordinary" Germans and developments at the grassroots, see A.I. Port, *Conflict and Stability in the German Democratic Republic* (Cambridge University Press, 2007); E. Sheffer, *Burned Bridge: How East and West Germans Made the Iron Curtain* (Oxford University Press, 2014); P. Major, *Behind the Berlin Wall: East Germany and the Frontiers of Power* (Oxford University Press, 2010); M. Allinson, *Politics and Popular Opinion in East Germany, 1945–1968* (Manchester University Press, 2000); P. Betts, *Within Walls: Private Life in the German Democratic Republic* (Oxford University Press, 2010); A. Merritt and R. Merritt, *Public Opinion in Occupied Germany: The OMGUS Surveys, 1945–1949* (University of Illinois Press, 1970).

Women, family, and sexuality are the subjects of R. Moeller, *Protecting Motherhood: Women and the Family in the Politics of Postwar West Germany* (University of California Press, 1993); D. Harsch, *Revenge of the Domestic: Women, the Family, and Communism in the German Democratic Republic* (Princeton University Press, 2006);

J. McLellan, *Love in the Time of Communism: Intimacy and Sexuality in the GDR* (Cambridge University Press, 2011); S. Clowes Huneke, *States of Liberation: Gay Men between Dictatorship and Democracy in Cold War Germany* (University of Toronto Press, 2022); C. Whisnant, *Male Homosexuality in West Germany: Between Persecution and Freedom, 1945–69* (Palgrave Macmillan, 2012).

There are a number of engaging studies on youth protest, the "sixty-eight" generation, and the emergence of an "alternative milieu." Besides the relevant chapters in M. Klimke and J. Scharloth, eds., *1968 in Europe: A History of Protest and Activism, 1956–1977* (Palgrave Macmillan, 2008), see C. von Hodenberg, *The Other '68: A Social History of West Germany's Revolt* (Oxford University Press, 2024); A. von der Goltz, *The Other '68ers: Student Protest and Christian Democracy in West Germany* (Oxford University Press, 2021); J. Häberlen, *The Emotional Politics of the Alternative Left: West Germany, 1968–1984* (Cambridge University Press, 2018); T. Brown, *West Germany and the Global Sixties: The Anti-Authoritarian Revolt, 1962–1978* (Cambridge University Press, 2013); Q. Slobodian, *Foreign Front: Third World Politics in Sixties West Germany* (Duke University Press, 2012); M. Fenemore, *Sex, Thugs and Rock 'n' Roll: Teenage Rebels in Cold-War East Germany* (Berghahn Books, 2007).

On domestic terrorism, see S. Aust, *Baader-Meinhof: The Inside Story of the R.A.F.* (Oxford University Press, 2009); J. Varon, *Bringing the War Home: The Weather Underground, the Red Army Faction, and Revolutionary Violence in the Sixties and Seventies* (University of California Press, 2004); P. Melzer, *Death in the Shape of a Young Girl: Women's Political Violence in the Red Army Faction* (NYU Press, 2015).

German "memory politics" and the legacy of the two German dictatorships have also garnered a great deal of popular and scholarly attention. See C. Maier, *The Unmasterable Past: History, Holocaust, and German National Identity* (Harvard University Press, 1988); R. Evans, *In Hitler's Shadow: West German Historians and the Attempt to Escape from the Nazi Past* (Pantheon, 1989); *Forever in the Shadow of Hitler? Original Documents of The* Historikerstreit, *the Controversy Concerning the Singularity of the Holocaust* (Humanities Press, 1993); R. Moeller, *War Stories: The Search for a Usable*

Past in the Federal Republic of Germany (University of California Press, 2001); J. Herf, *Divided Memory: The Nazi Past in the Two Germanys* (Harvard University Press, 1997); H. Harrison, *After the Berlin Wall: Memory and the Making of the New Germany, 1989 to the Present* (Cambridge University Press, 2019); D. Pendas, *The Frankfurt Auschwitz Trial, 1963–1965: Genocide, History, and the Limits of the Law* (Cambridge University Press, 2005); A.I. Port, *Never Again: Germans and Genocide After the Holocaust* (The Belknap Press of Harvard University Press, 2023).

Specifically on the GDR, see A. Saunders and D. Pinfold, eds., *Remembering and Rethinking the GDR: Multiple Perspectives and Plural Authenticities* (Palgrave Macmillan, 2012); A. Beattie, *Playing Politics with History: The Bundestag Inquiries into East Germany* (Berghahn Books, 2008); P. Cooke, *Representing East Germany Since Unification: From Colonization to Nostalgia* (Berg, 2005).

On the lot of migrants and other minorities, see D. Papademetriou and D. Klusmeyer, *Immigration Policy in the Federal Republic of Germany: Negotiating Membership and Remaking the Nation* (Berghahn Books, 2009); D. Gözturk, D. Gramling, and A. Kaes, eds., *Germany in Transit: Nation and Migration, 1955–2005* (University of California Press, 2007); L. Stokes, *Fear of the Family: Guest Workers and Family Migration in the Federal Republic of Germany* (Oxford University Press, 2022); R. Chin, *The Guest Worker Question in Postwar Germany* (Cambridge University Press, 2007). Also see E. Özyürek, *Subcontractors of Guilt: Holocaust Memory and Muslim Belonging in Postwar Germany* (Stanford University Press, 2023); T. Florvil, *Mobilizing Black Germany: Afro-German Women and the Making of a Transnational Movement* (University of Illinois Press, 2020).

The fall of the Berlin Wall, the collapse of state socialism, and the run-up to German unification have spurred a growth industry. Good places to start are C. Maier, *Dissolution: The Crisis of Communism and the End of East Germany* (Princeton University Press, 1997); K. Jarausch, *The Rush to German Unity* (Oxford University Press, 1994); C. Joppke, *East German Dissidents and the Revolution of 1989: Social Movement in a Leninist Regime* (NYU Press, 1994); S. Pfaff, *Exit-Voice Dynamics and the Collapse of East Germany: The Crisis of Leninism and the Revolution of 1989* (Duke University Press, 2006); D. Philipsen, *We Were the People: Voices from East Germany's Revolutionary Autumn of 1989* (Duke University Press, 1992); J.-W. Müller, *Another Country: German Intellectuals, Unification, and National Identity* (Yale University Press, 2000).

On high-level politics and German unification, see P. Zelikow and C. Rice, *Germany Unified and Europe Transformed: A Study in Statecraft* (Harvard University Press, 1995); S. Szabo, *The Diplomacy of German Unification* (Palgrave Macmillan, 1992); M.E. Sarotte, *The Collapse: The Accidental Opening of the Berlin Wall* (Basic Books, 2014). More specialized accounts include P. Quint, *The Imperfect Union: Constitutional Structures of German Unification* (Princeton University Press, 1997); G. Sinn and H.-W. Sinn, *Jumpstart: The Economic Unification of Germany* (MIT Press, 1992). For developments closer to the ground, see D. Berdahl, *Where the World Ended: Re-Unification and Identity in the German Borderland* (University of California Press, 1999).

The study of unified Germany is still in its infancy, but there are already good places to begin: C. Lemke and H. Welsh, *Germany Today: Politics and Policies in a Changing World* (Rowman & Littlefield, 2017); K. Jarausch, ed., *United Germany: Debating Processes and Prospects* (Berghahn Books, 2013); H. Maull, ed., *Germany's Uncertain Power: Foreign Policy of the Berlin Republic* (Palgrave Macmillan, 2006); P. Katzenstein, ed., *Tamed Power: Germany in Europe* (Cornell University Press, 1998); S. Szabo, *Germany, Russia, and the Rise of Geo-Economics* (Bloomsbury, 2015). On political extremism, see G. Braunthal, *Right-Wing Extremism in Contemporary Germany* (Palgrave Macmillan, 2009); E. Adaire, *Neo-Nazi Postmodern: Right-Wing Terror Tactics, the Intellectual New Right, and the Destabilization of Memory in Germany since 1989* (Bloomsbury, 2024); J. Kushner, *Look Away: A True Story of Murders, Bombings, and a Far-Right Campaign to Rid Germany of Immigrants* (Grand Central, 2024).

Superb websites that provide access to useful primary sources, many in English, include "German History in Documents and Images" (https://germanhistorydocs.ghi-dc.org/index.html); "German History Maps" (https://storymaps.arcgis.com/stories/e9cb1f0b7c9342498eebbfdc7bf5cf75); "German Propaganda Archive" (https://research.calvin.edu/german-propaganda-archive/).

Notes

Introduction

1 Richard Bessel, "Why Did the Weimar Republic Collapse?" in *Weimar: Why Did German Democracy Fail?* ed. Ian Kershaw (New York: St. Martin's Press, 1990), 148.
2 Charles S. Maier, "How Did Germany Go Right?" *Central European History* 51, no. 1 (2018): 134–6.
3 Hans-Ulrich Wehler, "Why Germany Must Remain Divided," Hoyt Lecture, Yale University, New Haven, CT, February 28, 1989.
4 A.J.P. Taylor, *The Course of German History: A Survey of the Development and History of Germany since 1815* (London: Routledge, 2000), 71.
5 For the relevant passage from Bismarck's 1862 "Blood and Iron" speech, see https://germanhistorydocs.ghi-dc.org/sub_document.cfm?document_id=250&language=english.
6 Carl E. Schorske, *Fin-de-Siècle Vienna: Politics and Culture* (New York: Knopf, 1980), 116–80.
7 For the best-known use of the phrase "place in the sun," see https://germanhistorydocs.ghi-dc.org/pdf/eng/607_Buelow_Place%20in%20the%20Sun_111.pdf.
8 For the text of Wilhelm's speech, see https://www.1000dokumente.de/Dokumente/Thronrede_Kaiser_Wilhelms_II._vor_den_Reichstagsabgeordneten; on "*Flucht nach vorne*," see Hans-Ulrich Wehler, *Das Deutsche Kaiserreich, 1871–1918* (Göttingen: Vandenhoeck & Ruprecht, 1977), 207.
9 For an expert exploration of these issues, see Ian Kershaw, *The Nazi Dictatorship: Problems and Perspectives of Interpretation*, 4th ed. (London: Bloomsbury, 2000).

Chapter 1: Defeat (1945–1949)

1 John Maynard Keynes, *The Economic Consequences of the Peace* (London: Routledge, 2003).
2 Cited in Andrew I. Port, *Conflict and Stability in the German Democratic Republic* (New York: Cambridge University Press, 2007), 118.
3 Joseph Stalin, "Order of the Day, No. 55," February 23, 1942 (https://www.marxists.org/reference/archive/stalin/works/1942/02/23.htm).
4 Cited in Manfred Görtemaker, *Geschichte der Bundesrepublik Deutschland: Von der Gründung bis zur Gegenwart* (Munich: Beck, 1999), 66.
5 Wilfried Loth, *Stalin's Unwanted Child: The Soviet Union, the German Question and the Founding of the GDR*, trans. Robert F. Hogg (Basingstoke: Palgrave Macmillan, 1998); the original German title was *Stalins unbeliebtes Kind* (Stalin's unloved child).
6 Hans-Ulrich Wehler, *Deutsche Gesellschaftsgeschichte 1949–1990* (Munich: Beck, 2008), xv.

Chapter 2: Revival (1949–1961)

1 Fritz René Allemann, *Bonn ist nicht Weimar* (Cologne: Kiepenheuer & Witsch, 1956).
2 Ludwig Erhard, *Wohlstand für Alle* (Düsseldorf: Econ-Verlag, 1957).
3 See Michael Wildt, *Am Beginn der "Konsumgesellschaft": Mangelerfahrung, Lebenshaltung, Wohlstandshoffnung in Westdeutschland in den fünfziger Jahren* (Hamburg: Ergebnisse-Verlag, 1994).
4 See Uta Poiger, *Jazz, Rock, and Rebels: Cold War Politics and American Culture in a Divided Germany* (Berkeley: University of California Press, 2000).
5 See Jeffrey Herf, *Divided Memory: The Nazi Past in the Two Germanys* (Cambridge, MA: Harvard University Press, 1997), 106–61.
6 See Peter Ruggenthaler, "The 1952 Stalin Note on German

Unification: The Ongoing Debate," *Journal of Cold War Studies* 13, no. 4 (2011): 172–212.

7 In 1922, Germany and the USSR, the two main pariah states of post-World War I Europe, signed a major bilateral treaty during an international conference held in Rapallo, Italy. The term "Rapallo" came to be associated in the West with some sort of devious Soviet–German conspiracy to dominate Europe.

8 Seth Givens and Ingo Trauschweizer, eds., *Berlin and the Cold War* (Athens: Ohio University Press, 2024), 2.

9 On this concept, see Pierre Nora, "Between Memory and History: *Les Lieux de Mémoire*," *Representations* 26 (1989): 7–24.

10 See the text of the manifesto at https://www.uni-goettingen.de/en/the+manifesto/54320.html.

11 Helmut Schelsky, *Die skeptische Generation: Eine Soziologie der deutschen Jugend* (Düsseldorf: Eugen Diedrichs, 1963).

12 Historians of Germany (misleadingly) use the term "zero hour" (*Stunde null*) to suggest an absolute break with the past in 1945.

13 Port, *Conflict and Stability*, 142.

14 Andrew I. Port, "Democracy and Dictatorship in the Cold War: The Two Germanies, 1949–1961," in *The Oxford Handbook of Modern German History*, ed. Helmut W. Smith (Oxford: Oxford University Press, 2011), 615.

Chapter 3: Consolidation (1961–1972)

1 See, for example, Dietrich Staritz, *Geschichte der DDR 1949–1985*, rev. ed. (Frankfurt am Main: Suhrkamp, 1996), 196.

2 Peter Bender, "Panzer am Checkpoint Charlie," *Die Zeit*, November 25, 1988 (https://www.zeit.de/1988/48/panzer-am-checkpoint-charlie/komplettansicht).

3 See David Schoenbaum, *The* Spiegel *Affair* (New York: Doubleday, 1968).

4 Werner Barm, "Die Parole Überholen, ohne Einzuholen," *Die Welt*, July 30, 1970 (https://ghdi.ghi-dc.org/pdf/deu/Chapter9Doc%205.pdf).

5 See Jonathan Zatlin, *The Currency of Socialism: Money and Political Culture in East Germany* (New York: Cambridge University Press, 2007), 203–42.
6 Stefan Wolle, *Die heile Welt der Diktatur: Alltag und Herrschaft in der DDR, 1971–1989* (Berlin: Ch. Links Verlag, 1998), 34.
7 See, for example, Jörg Roesler, *Zwischen Plan und Markt: Die Wirtschaftsreform in der DDR, 1963–1970* (Freiburg/Breisgau: Haufe, 1990); Hermann Graml, "Die Legende von der verpaßten Gelegenheit: Zur sowjetischen Notenkampagne des Jahres 1952," *Vierteljahrshefte für Zeitgeschichte* 29, no. 3 (1981): 307–41.
8 John Kenneth Galbraith, *The Affluent Society* (Boston: Houghton Mifflin, 1958).
9 See Andrew Arato and Eike Gebhardt, eds., *The Essential Frankfurt School Reader* (London: Bloomsbury, 1982).
10 "Regierungserklärung von Bundeskanzler Willy Brandt vor dem Deutschen Bundestag in Bonn am 28. Oktober 1969" (https://www.willy-brandt-biografie.de/wp-content/uploads/2017/08/Regierungserklaerung_Willy_Brandt_1969.pdf).
11 Egon Bahr, "Wandel durch Annäherung [Tutzinger Rede]," July 15, 1963 (https://www.1000dokumente.de/Dokumente/Egon_Bahr,_Wandel_durch_Ann%c3%a4herung_(Tutzinger_Rede)).
12 "Regierungserklärung von Bundeskanzler Willy Brandt."
13 "Text of Brandt's TV Talk From Soviet to Germans," *New York Times*, August 13, 1970 (https://www.nytimes.com/1970/08/13/archives/text-of-brandts-tv-talk-from-soviet-to-germans.html).
14 Walter Isaacson, "Is One Germany Better Than Two?" *Time*, November 20, 1989 (https://time.com/archive/6703900/is-one-germany-better-than-two/).
15 For the text of the 1974 constitution, see https://www.verfassungen.de/ddr/verf74.htm.
16 See, for example, Herbert Meißner, *Konvergenztheorie und Realität* (Berlin: Akademie-Verlag, 1969).
17 See Jan-Werner Müller, *Verfassungspatriotismus* (Frankfurt am Main: Suhrkamp, 2010).

Chapter 4: Crisis (1973–1989)

1 See Kay Schiller and Chris Young, *The 1972 Munich Olympics and the Making of Modern Germany* (Berkeley: University of California Press, 2010).

2 Jean Fourastié, *Les Trente Glorieuses, ou la Révolution invisible de 1946 à 1975* (Paris: Fayard, 1979).

3 For an English translation of the speech, see https://www.bundespraesident.de/SharedDocs/Downloads/DE/Reden/2015/02/150202-RvW-Rede-8-Mai-1985-englisch.pdf?__blob=publicationFile. On the "historians' controversy," see *Forever in the Shadow of Hitler? Original Documents of the Historikerstreit*, trans. James Knowlton and Truett Cates (Atlantic Highlands, NJ: Humanities Press, 1993).

4 For the text of this article in English, see https://www.gesetze-im-internet.de/englisch_gg/englisch_gg.html.

5 It also led to the rise of the *Republikaner* (Republicans), an extreme-right, xenophobic party that enjoyed some electoral success in the 1980s and 1990s and was led by Franz Schönhuber, a former Nazi and voluntary member of the Waffen-SS during World War II.

6 Peter Bender, *Deutschlands Wiederkehr: Eine ungeteilte Nachkriegsgeschichte, 1945–1990* (Stuttgart: Klett-Cotta, 2007), 210.

7 Ulrich Plenzdorf, *The New Sorrows of Young W.*, trans. Romy Fursland (London: Pushkin Press, 2015), 26.

8 Wolle, *Die heile Welt*, 217–19; Wehler, *Deutsche Gesellschaftsgeschichte*, 79.

9 Erich Honecker, *Bericht des Politbüros an die 11. Tagung des Zentralkomitees der SED* (Berlin: Dietz, 1965).

10 Rudolf Bahro, *The Alternative in Eastern Europe*, trans. David Fernbach (London: NLB, 1978).

11 For the text of the Berlin Appeal, see https://ghdi.ghi-dc.org/sub_document.cfm?document_id=1134#:~:text=Since%20a%20nuclear%20war%20affords,of%20psychological%20preparation%20for%20war.

12 https://ghdi.ghi-dc.org/sub_document.cfm?document_id=1146&language=german; also see Ulrich Herbert, *A*

History of Twentieth-Century Germany, trans. Ben Fowkes (New York: Oxford University Press, 2019), 878.

13 Wehler, "Why Germany Must Remain Divided"; for Kohl's remarks, see https://www.bundeskanzler-helmut-kohl.de/seite/07-september/.

Chapter 5: Dis-Unity (1989–1998)

1 Footage of the entire press conference can be viewed at https://www.youtube.com/watch?v=UN3pY_EJ7_8.

2 Bender, *Deutschlands Wiederkehr*, 235–6.

3 See Kohl's Ten-Point Plan at https://germanhistorydocs.ghi-dc.org/pdf/eng/chapter1_doc10english.pdf.

4 See Jürgen Habermas, *Die nachholende Revolution* (Frankfurt am Main: Suhrkamp, 1990).

5 See Andrew I. Port, "'There Will Be Blood': The Violent Underside of the 'Peaceful' East German Revolution of 1989," in *Tel Aviver Jahrbuch für deutsche Geschichte*, ed. José Brunner, Doron Avraham, and Marianne Zepp (Göttingen: Wallstein, 2014), 217–35.

6 For Reagan's remarks, see https://www.reaganfoundation.org/media/128814/brandenburg.pdf.

7 Alexis de Tocqueville, *The Old Regime and the French Revolution*, trans. Stuart Gilbert (New York: Doubleday, 1956).

8 On this controversial issue, see Mary Elise Sarotte, "A Broken Promise? What the West Really Told Moscow About NATO Expansion," *Foreign Affairs* 93, no. 5 (2014): 90–7.

9 Robert J. McCartney, "Kohl's Comment Sets Off Diplomatic Contretemps," *Washington Post*, October 25, 1986.

10 For Kohl's remarks, see https://ghdi.ghi-dc.org/sub_document.cfm?document_id=3101.

11 See, for example, Dirk Oschmann, *Der Osten: Eine westdeutsche Erfindung* (Berlin: Ullstein, 2023).

12 Sidney Verba and Gabriel Almond, *The Civic Culture: Political Attitudes and Democracy in Five Nations* (Princeton, NJ: Princeton University Press, 1963).

13 For the arguments presented in this section, see Andrew I. Port, *Never Again: Germans and Genocide After the Holocaust*

(Cambridge, MA: The Belknap Press of Harvard University Press, 2023). Also see Peter Katzenstein, ed., *Tamed Power: Germany in Europe* (Ithaca, NY: Cornell University Press, 1997).

14 Wolf Biermann, "Kriegshetze, Friedenshetze," *Die Zeit*, February 1, 1991.

15 Quoted in Karin Johnston, "German Public Opinion and the Crisis in Bosnia," in *International Public Opinion and the Bosnia Crisis*, ed. Richard Sobel and Eric Shiraev (Lanham, MD: Lexington Books, 2003), 259.

16 Quoted in Ulrich Krotz, *History and Foreign Policy in France and Germany* (Basingstoke: Palgrave Macmillan, 2015), 131.

17 Cited in Port, *Never Again*, 274.

18 See the text of the decision at https://www.bundesverfassungsgericht.de/SharedDocs/Pressemitteilungen/DE/1994/bvg94-029.html.

19 The book appeared almost simultaneously in German translation: *Hitlers willige Vollstrecker: Ganz gewöhnliche Deutsche und der Holocaust*, trans. Klaus Kochmann (Berlin: Siedler, 1996).

20 Martin Walser, *Friedenspreis des Deutschen Buchhandels 1998: Ansprachen aus Anlaß der Verleihung* (Frankfurt am Main: Buchhändler-Vereinigung, 1998), 46. Also see Hamburger Institut für Sozialforschung, *Verbrechen der Wehrmacht: Dimensionen des Vernichtungskrieges 1941 bis 1944* (Hamburg: Hamburger Edition, 2021).

21 See Gavriel D. Rosenfeld, *The Fourth Reich: The Specter of Nazism from World War II to the Present* (New York: Cambridge University Press, 2019).

22 See the text of the treaty at https://eur-lex.europa.eu/legal-content/EN/TXT/PDF/?uri=CELEX:11992M/TXT&from=EN.

Chapter 6: Normality? (1998–2024)

1 See "'Immer an der Grenze des Konflikts,'" *Der Spiegel*, February 19, 1978.

2 For Schröder's remarks, see Deutscher Bundestag, Stenographischer Bericht, 186. Sitzung, 14. Wahlperiode (September 12, 2001), 18, 293. Also see "Rede des

Bundesministers der Verteidigung, Dr. Peter Struck," December 20, 2002 (https://www.bundesregierung.de/breg-de/service/newsletter-und-abos/bulletin/rede-des-bundes ministers-der-verteidigung-dr-peter-struck--784328); William Noah Glucroft, "Germany Rethinks its Military Missions," *Deutsche Welle*, August 19, 2021 (https://www.dw.com/en/after-afghanistan-germany-rethinks-its-military-missions/a-58912418).
3 "Schröder macht Irak zum Wahlkampfthema," *Die Welt*, August 6, 2002.
4 See Bassam Tibi, *Europa ohne Identität? Die Krise der multikulturellen Gesellschaft* (Munich: Bertelsmann 2000), 154.
5 See, for example, Sunny Hundal, "Angela Merkel is Now the Leader of the Free World, Not Donald Trump," *The Independent* (UK), February 1, 2017.
6 Siobhan Dowling, "There's No Getting Around It, Germany Is Taking Over Europe," *Business Insider*, November 19, 2011 (https://web.archive.org/web/20120502031204/http://articles.businessinsider.com/2011-11-19/europe/30418846_1_euro-zone-euro-crisis-german-power).
7 The phrase was originally used in a different context. See Timothy Garton Ash, *In Europe's Name: Germany and the Divided Continent* (New York: Random House, 1993).
8 For footage of her remarks at a press conference held on August 31, 2015, see https://www.youtube.com/watch?v=k-DQki0MMFh4.
9 https://www.ibtimes.co.uk/germany-anti-islam-pegida-pro test-rally-draws-record-25000-dresden-1483097.
10 Deutscher Bundestag, Stenographischer Bericht, 19. Sitzung, 20. Wahlperiode (February 27, 2022), 1350–4.

Epilogue

1 Ulrich Zawatka-Gerlach, "Helmut Kohl wieder zu Gast vorm Rathaus Schöneberg," *Tagesspiegel*, August 28, 2002.
2 According to surveys conducted that year, four-fifths of West Germans did not believe that unification was likely in the next thirty years. See Bender, *Deutschlands Wiederkehr*, 204.
3 For the full text of the speech, see https://foreignpolicy.

com/2025/02/18/vance-speech-munich-full-text-read-transcript-europe/.

4 The Epilogue was completed on February 25, 2025, and this sentence amended on May 8.

5 Robert Kagan, "The New German Question," *Foreign Affairs* (May/June 2019): 108–17.

6 This was widely reported in the media. See, for example, Michael Gold, "Trump Says He Gave NATO Allies Warning: Pay In or He'd Urge Russian Aggression," *New York Times*, February 10, 2024 (https://www.nytimes.com/2024/02/10/us/politics/trump-nato-russia.html).

7 For footage of Merz's comments, see https://www.youtube.com/watch?v=tZy7D2u2tGI.

Index